EV*L*...*ING ®

WINE
MINI BOOK

Danny May and Andy Sharpe

Adams Media Corporation
Holbrook, Massachusetts

An Everything® Series Book.
"Everything" is a registered trademark of Adams Media Corporation.

Published by Adams Media Corporation
260 Center Street, Holbrook, MA 02343
www.adamsmedia.com

ISBN: 1-58062-498-7

Printed in Canada.

J I H G F E D C B A

Library of Congress Cataloging-in-Publication Data
available from the publisher.

This publication is designed to provide accurate and authorita-
tive information with regard to the subject matter covered. It is
sold with the understanding that the publisher is not engaged in
rendering legal, accounting, or other professional advice. If legal
advice or other expert assistance is required, the services of a
competent professional person should be sought.
— From a *Declaration of Principles* jointly adopted by a Committee of the
American Bar Association and a Committee of Publishers and Associations

Illustrations by Barry Littmann.

*This book is available at quantity discounts for bulk purchases.
For information, call 1-800-872-5627.*

GENERAL OFFICE
ENVIRONMENTS
www.goeinc.com

&

Kimball®Office

We Value
Our
Relationship
With You

Contents

Chapter 2

Wine and Food 🍷 51

Chapter 3

Varietal Wines, Grape by Grape 🍇 71

Chapter 4

Special Occasion Wines ✦ 161

Introduction

Learning about wine is, for many people, an important rite of passage into adulthood—an enjoyable experience with many benefits. Your journey through the world of wine will take you around the globe, from California to Australia and beyond. You will become familiar with a broad range of styles of wine and find among them your favorites. As you learn to pair wine and food, your newfound appreciation of good wine will add an extra dimension to the pleasures of the table, as well. The ability to enjoy a good wine is an acquired one—and its own reward.

The vast array of wines offered by merchants can be intimidating to a wine novice. To many beginners, wine labels do more harm than good, as far as describing the contents within. Some wines are labeled according to their region of origin; some are labeled by grape variety; and still others are sold under brand names. "Wine talk" is another common obstacle. The terminology used to describe wines can be difficult to understand, and often proves to be very subjective. This confusion can lead to a bad experience with a wine purchase. As you learn about wine, you will quickly find that these pitfalls are easily avoidable. It's simple, really—read about wines, taste them, and take note of what you like and dislike.

Buying and tasting wines yourself can be an expensive undertaking. Fortunately, many wine shops offer tastings on weekends, which are a lot of fun. Arranging group tastings is a cost-effective way to sample several different wines of your own choosing.

Although we discuss wines ranging in price from $3 to $500, the goal of this book is to allow you to enjoy as many types of wine as possible that sell for no more than $10 per bottle. Accordingly, and with the novice in mind, we focus mainly on the inexpensive and moderately expensive wines.

Before you set out on your journey, here are some tips to enhance your wine-drinking experience.

- Let your wine breathe if it needs to. Ten minutes often goes a long way.
- Use crystal wine glasses to add to the ambience.

- Have some food in your stomach so you don't get "buzzed" prematurely.
- Have a glass of water readily available, and don't be thirsty when you drink wine.
- Keep the wine in your mouth long enough to really taste it. Don't be afraid to move it around with your tongue.
- Don't drink your wine, especially white, so slowly that it warms up too much.
- Drink wine with good and appropriate food.

Whether you're a beginner or a wine connoisseur, the tips and suggestions included in this book will help you to identify wines you might like to try. So bon voyage, and cheers!

CHAPTER 1

Buying Wine

U nless you set out for the wine store with a specific bottle of wine in mind, you will have to make a buying decision based on limited information. Your goal is to bring home a wine you will like, at a price you feel comfortable with. In the end you may end up with a bottle you've had in the past because this was the most informed selection you could make.

When you buy a bottle of wine, you don't want to buy damaged goods. Since there are no tires to kick, you need to use other tests.

1. Is the bottle filled up? This used to be more of an issue in the less industrial days of wine bottling. See how high the wine is in the neck of the wine bottle compared to other bottles. There is no need to pay the same for less.

2. Feel the cork through the plastic wrapper on the top of the bottle. The cork shouldn't feel pushed in or out. The top of the cork should be close to flush with the top of the bottle. Cork movement can be indicative of a bad cork or a wine that has been exposed to temperature extremes.

3. Hold the bottle up to the light. Is it clear or murky? Only in an older wine is it okay to see sediment.

Wine from the same "batch" should be the same color. If you can't figure out which color is the right color, buy a different wine.

Before you buy wine at a store, you should be convinced that the store is kept at cool temperatures twenty-four hours a day. You also don't want to buy wines that are stored in a place where they get a lot of light or are exposed to a radiator.

Assuming you can't get any good information from a store worker or display, here are some good tips:

Know a Grape:
If you like Sauvignon Blanc but can't find your favorite bottle,

you may want to try a bottle from a different producer.

Know a Region: If the Cabernet you like is from Alexander Valley, California, try a different Cabernet from that same region. Climate and soil, *terroir,* play a big part in winemaking.

Know a Producer: If you like Pride Mountain Merlot, you may like Pride Mountain Cabernet Sauvignon, since the two wines are made by the same person, or at least with the same philosophy.

If you have enough interest in wine you owe it to yourself to attend a free wine tasting, which are often held at wine stores. Certainly, tasting a wine without having first to buy it is a worthwhile opportunity.

The Safest Wines to Buy

Although this book attempts to demystify wine, there are way too many wine-buying options and wine-making parameters to make buying wine a no-brainer. Even if you find a wine you like, when stock of that vintage runs out you may be searching for a new wine. Many wines taste different from vintage to vintage.

If you buy wines with labels printed in English and the grape variety or varieties in the wine are denoted, you will at least know a few things about your potential purchase, like what the heck you're buying. Not only will you have some idea of what you are buying, but after you drink the wine you can look at the bottle and know what type of wine you just did or didn't enjoy.

Because Australia and California have good grape-growing weather most years, and wine from both places is labeled in nothing but English, buying wines from these two countries is the best place for wine beginners to start. But don't get the impression these wines are better than wines from other regions.

If you are buying California jug wines, they are going to be the same every year. These wines get a bad rap from wine snobs. If you need a lot of wine, these large commercial wines are an excellent choice. But chances are, if you are reading this book, you want your tastes to branch out into less familiar territory.

Australian red wines that are exported to North America may be the safest red-wine bet around. These wines tend to be accessible without being overly simple. The white wines from Australia, especially the blends of Semillon and Chardonnay, tend to be crowd pleasers. Straight Chardonnay is a fairly safe bet, although some versions could be considered too fruity for the dinner table.

Again, since the wine's grape variety or varieties are printed on the label, it will be easy to reproduce a positive Australian wine experience, even if you can't find the same bottle the next time you buy wine in a store or order it in a restaurant. Australia exports a lot of good, easy-to-drink, inexpensive red and white wines, and keeps things easy for consumers, since they don't seem to export many bad bottles.

Chardonnays from large California producers that sell in the $10–$13 range are a very safe bet. Chardonnay is an easy grape to grow in the California climate. The big producers have the formula down pat. They grow some Chardonnay grapes; they buy some other Chardonnay grapes from other vineyards; they have a goal—their Chardonnay formula; and they always reach that goal.

Beaujolais Nouveau ("new wine" from the French region of Beaujolais) is an easy red wine to buy. Although the label doesn't say so, all of this wine comes from the Gamay grape. It is meant to be consumed right away, so you won't have to worry that the wine you are buying is too young. All of its producers make Beaujolais in a light, simple, fruity, good-with-food style. These wines are also consistent from year to year. Best of all, they are cheap: Good ones can be had for $7. The very best, the cru Beaujolais, sell for under $15. This is a terrific red wine to serve to people who think they only like white wine.

Pinot Gris (or Pinot Grigio, as it is called in Italy) is a white wine that is very easy to drink and to match with food. Powerfully spiced foods can overwhelm this somewhat timid wine, but it goes well with a wide variety of pastas, seafood, and lighter chicken dishes.

Another good way to get a good wine is by sticking with producers whose wines are generally good and widely available. This may be the best way to venture into European wines. Reliable European producers include Louis Latour (France), Ruffino (Italy), and Montecillo (Spain).

Risky Wine Purchases

What can go wrong when you buy a bottle of wine?

You can buy wine that is just plain lousy. Some wines, like some movies, just shouldn't have been made. Other wines may deserve to have been made, but like some movies, you just don't like them. If you have no idea what you like and/or have no idea what you are buying, you may end up with a good wine that you happen not to like.

If you are buying wine to be consumed with a meal, you can get into trouble with the "right wine at the wrong time" syndrome. The concept of buying *the* right wine is a silly one. When painting your house, you may look at a hundred color samples and pick *the* right one, but the wine-buying scenario is very different. There is a good chance you have never tasted the wine you are thinking of buying. If you have, you may not have had it with the food you are planning on serving.

What is the most likely scenario for buying a bad wine? Wines that are inexpensive or that have a label that boasts of a popular grape variety can often be bad wines. If a bottle of Chardonnay or Cabernet Sauvignon were of high quality, it wouldn't sell for $6. You are much better off trying a nonvarietal wine or a "lesser" variety at the low end of the price spectrum.

Now, if you have an idea of what wine grape varieties you like, buying a European wine can be difficult without help. If you find you like California Pinot Noir and are thinking of trying a French Pinot, you won't usually find the words "Pinot Noir" on the bottles of French wines you see at the liquor store. You need to develop an understanding of the cross-relationship between California varietals and French wine regions. Cheat sheets are allowed.

Older wines are difficult to buy. Some wines fade when they are aged too long; other older wines are still too young. You may see a fifteen-year-old bottle of wine that could easily be five years too young or five years too old.

Buying Wine for the Nonconnoisseur

If you are buying wine for a person who has only a casual interest in wine, chances are that person is going to drink the wine with a meal. Your goal is to buy a wine that is easy to like.

If you are buying wine for someone who likes white wine and who likes things that are familiar, then a California Chardonnay is a good choice. The wine is probably going to taste good, assuming you don't look for the cheapest California Chardonnay in the store. Also, there is nothing more familiar to the casual white-wine drinker than "California" and "Chardonnay." If there is a knowledgeable salesperson in the store, ask for a bottle that isn't too acidic or oaky; a $12 Chardonnay from California is a very safe bet.

If you want to give something a little less conventional in the white-wine area, an Italian Pinot Grigio costing $10–12 is a good choice for a lighter white wine. These wines are excellent with food. The Semillon/Chardonnay blends from Australia are also usually very good and fairly priced at $8–10.

When it comes to red wine, there is no sure thing equivalent to the white California Chardonnays. If you are trying to buy a red wine for a person who wants something familiar, you might try a Chianti from Italy, which matches very well with food. Chianti, thanks in part to the American jug wine named Chianti, has a lot of name recognition. Although decent $8 bottles are out there, you may want to improve your odds of getting a good bottle and spend $10.

If you want to buy a red wine for someone adventurous, your choices are vast. A Canadian Baco Noir is a very drinkable red wine. It's quite compatible with food but boring without it. A price of $8–10 will usually get you a good-tasting, unassuming Canadian red. French Beaujolais (Nouveau or not) wines from the Gamay grape are easy to buy

($8–10) and easy to drink. Many of the Beaujolais Nouveaus also come with a festive wine label.

Although it sounds ridiculous, you could buy a red wine with an interesting or funny

Consistently Good White Wines ($10 and under)

Sauvignon Blanc—Kronendaal (South Africa) $6
Chardonnay—Monterey (California) $7
Riesling—Schmitt Soehne (Germany) $7
Muscadet—Marcel Martin (France) $8
Sauvignon Blanc—Canyon Road (California) $8
Semillon/Chardonnay—Penfolds
Koonunga Hill (Australia) $8
Riesling—Bernkasteler Kurfurstlay Kabinett
(Germany) $9
Chardonnay—Meridien (California) $10
Pinot Grigio—Mezza Corona (Italy) $10
Saint-Véran—Louis Latour (France)
(It's Chardonnay!) $10

label and/or name. There are a lot of bottles for $10 and under to choose from in this category. If you buy a nonvarietal U.S. table wine, you are probably going to end up with a middle-of-the-road safe wine. If the person to whom you are giving the wine really doesn't know one grape from another, packaging may be the thing to look for.

For the Grateful Dead fan there are at least two California wines with names and labels inspired by the Grateful Dead, or at least targeting Grateful Dead fans. Look for Dead Red "Space Your Face" red table unwine (non-alcoholic) and Grateful Red, a Pinot Noir. These wines are crafted to be accessible—like the music? Expect to spend between $10 and $15 for such a wine: not cheap, but less than a ticket to a Dead Show.

Marilyn Merlot pairs a hot varietal with a popular icon, who appears in living color on the label. At $20, this wine may be worth more to you unopened.

If you are interested in spending upwards of $20 for a red, a California, celebrity-free Pinot Noir may be your best option. These wines are rich and fruity, and easily appreciated by wine novices and veterans alike.

Buying Wine for the Connoisseur

If you are going to buy wine as a gift for a connoisseur, and you are not a connoisseur, you have a couple of good options. If the gift is for someone who takes pride in his or her roots, try to buy a good bottle from that person's homeland. Good bottles of wine are produced in countries such as Israel, New Zealand, Canada, and Switzerland, to name a few. South Africa is not the only country in Africa that produces wine. Morocco, Algeria, and even Egypt make wine. Such purchases may require some research, but a knowledgeable wine salesperson, or possibly the Internet, can point you in the right direction. A $20–30 bottle is apt be good, and spending any more for a wine of unknown quality is foolish.

Another approach is to buy a "best-of type" with a reasonable price tag. The best wines from the famous regions of the world are going to cost you a couple of hundred dollars. However, the best wines from Chile, Oregon, or the underappreciated Alsace region of France will cost you far less. For example, $30 will buy you an excellent Riesling from Alsace. The premium French *cru* Beaujolais wines won't kill you financially. These wines are especially good for people who live in warm climates or who entertain a lot.

Consistently Good Red Wines ($10 and under)
Merlot—Dulong (France) $6
Cabernet Sauvignon—Santa Rita (Chile) $6
Beaujolais-Villages—Louis Jadot (France) $9
Shiraz—Hardy's Nottage Hill (Australia) $9
Rioja—Bodegas Monticillo (Spain) $9
Zinfandel—Rosenblum (California) $10
Pinot Noir—Firesteed (Oregon) $10
Shiraz—Lindemans Bin 50 (Australia) $10
Cabernet Sauvignon—Dunnewood (California) $10
Chianti—Castello di Quercetto (Italy) $10

Buying a magnum (double-sized bottle) of good wine is another offbeat but sensible idea. The wine itself may not wow the connoisseur, but these bottles look impressive at any dinner table. Expect to spend $35–50 for a magnum capable of impressing a connoisseur.

Wine for People Who Don't Like Wine

What qualities in wine do some people find objectionable? Three, usually—acidity, tannin, and alcohol.

Wine is the most acidic beverage we consume. The acids in wine are balanced in part by its fruit and sugar. In dry wines, those with little or no residual sugar, the acidity can be overwhelming. Acidic wines are often described as "food wines," mainly because they

can be best appreciated with food already in your mouth. Starches such as bread, rice, or pasta provide balance to the acidity.

So, the answer is to find wines low in acidity. Most American rosés fit into this category, as do Australian Chardonnays. French Beaujolais (made from Gamay grapes) is the red wine that is most likely to be acceptable to a person who doesn't like the acidity of wine.

For those who dislike the strong taste of alcohol, there are two wonderful types of wine to enjoy. Moscato d'Asti is a low-alcohol, slightly sparkling wine from Northern Italy. At 5.5 percent alcohol, half that of normal wine, its subtle floral components shine through. Only slightly higher in alcohol is late-harvest, somewhat sweet German Riesling, which can be exquisitely rich (and a somewhat expensive gift for someone who claims not to like wine).

Red Wine for People Who Don't Like Red Wine

Don't waste big bucks on red wine for someone who claims to hate it. Cheaper red wines tend to be more offensive than cheaper whites. Since most people start off drinking inexpensive wine, it makes sense that a lot of them write off red wine during their formative wine-drinking years.

Look for low-tannin wines. Beaujolais, from the southern Burgundy region of France, is a fruity, crowd-pleasing, gulping wine. This Gamay-based wine may be the strongest argument against red-wine prejudice. Australian blends of Cabernet Sauvignon and Shiraz show enough raisiny fruit to put the tannin in its place for under $12. For $11–15, California Pinot Noir, thick with glycerine and unctuous fruit, converts many a red-wine skeptic. Rioja from Spain is another option.

If tannin isn't the problem, then maybe it's a yearning for fruit. California Pinot Noir is the fruitiest incarnation of the varietal. Red Zinfandel is also very fruity, but it may be too tannic to convince someone that red wine deserves another chance. If you choose a Pinot Noir, look for the rich and fruity Pinots that come from California, especially those from the Carneros and Santa Barbara regions. French Pinot Noir and those from Oregon and Washington tend to be more austere as they have less ripe fruit flavor.

White Wine for People
Who Don't Like White Wine

This one is difficult. If they say they don't like white wine, then they probably don't like typical California Chardonnay. White wine that is served chilled and that lacks tannin is generally a less complicated beverage, which, for many red-wine drinkers, translates into boring.

There are many directions to take:

1. Try good French Chardonnay—white Burgundy is less fruity and more acidic than most California and Australian Chardonnay.
2. Go weird with Viognier, the Rhône white with a personality so different from Chardonnay as to be unrecognizable to a Chardonnay drinker.

Viognier is growing in popularity with California winemakers.

3. Gewürztraminer, the Dennis Rodman of white grapes, is certainly worth a shot.

4. Best of all options may be a decent French Alsace or German Riesling. Less pungent than Gewürztraminer, Riesling is more flowery than fruity—again, different enough from Chardonnay that it is worth a try.

Wine Tasting

Professional tasters prefer a day-lit, odor-free room with white walls and tabletops to allow for optimum viewing of a wine's color without anything visually stimulating enough to distract one from the wine. Normal people enjoy tasting wine with friends at a dinner table and don't worry about the distractions of food smells and other niceties.

No matter where you conduct your tasting, make sure your wines are served at the right temperature. This is critical! Wines served too cold can't really be tasted. Those served too warm will seem out of balance. By this we mean a warm white wine may seem too sweet, while a warm red wine is apt to taste too acidic or alcoholic.

OBVIOUSLY A 1983 DOM DE CHEVALIER BORDEAUX FROM THE REGION OF THE UPPER GARONNE.

Remember that tasting is not a test—your subjective response is more important than any "right answers." The bottom line is: Wine that tastes good to you is good wine.

Below is the basic six-step process of wine tasting.

1. *Look at a wine:* Judging a wine's color allows you to make some assessment about how old a wine is and how heavy a wine might feel in your mouth. Young red wines are close to purple in color. Over time, they pass through red toward brown. White wines start off in various shades of clear and they head toward a straw color.

   Different wines have different colors. Cabernet Sauvignon is darker by nature than Sangiovese. Also, the riper the harvested grape, the more color it adds to a wine.

Judging density of color is where the strong light source and white background come in to play. Clear, clean glasses are also essential. Thickness of color usually indicates a richness, fruitiness, and/or heaviness. Thickness is best judged toward the edges of the wine as it sits in the glass. Glasses are tipped to a 45° angle to create a large edge of wine against the side of the glass. This means you don't want your glass much more than a quarter full during a critical tasting. The proper way to hold any wine glass is by the stem. This will keep smudges off the bowl so you can see your wine better and not influence its temperature with the warmth of your hand.

2. *Swirl the wine in the glass:* Swirling will help expose a wine to more oxygen, which could be a goal of the taster eager to taste a wine right out of the bottle, but is usually done to release aromas. Swirling is another reason to conservatively fill your wine glass. The tears of wine that slowly run down the side of the bowl after the swirling stops will evaporate quickly and release concentrated aromas.

   The easiest way to swirl a glass full of wine is to leave the base of the glass on the table. If you swirl your glass somewhat vigorously, you will create an invisible tornado of aromas that lift up and out of your wine glass.

3. *Smell the wine:* This is where all hell can break loose. Cries of "tar," "elder-

berries," "coconut," "coffee,"
"tobacco," and so on, are apt to be
uttered at a tasting. This may be the
most difficult aspect of a tasting for
the novice to swallow. The best way to
smell a wine is to stick your nose into
the glass. There is no getting around
this. If you aren't in a social setting
that will support this type of behavior,
at least bring the glass very close to
your nose.

4. *Taste It:* It is important to let the wine
linger in your mouth for at least ten
seconds; otherwise, you aren't really
tasting it. It's important to roll the
wine around your mouth with
your tongue, exposing it to as
much of your mouth as

possible. Serious tasters will open their lips a bit and inhale into their mouths while wine rests on the tongue. This encourages vaporization, which releases aroma and flavor.

5. *Swallow or Spit:* If you are at a dinner table, you are probably not going to be spitting out your experiments. However, if you go to a tasting where you sample a lot of wine, you are going to want to spit out most of the wines you try. Of course it is easier to judge a wine's aftertaste, known as its "finish," when you swallow it rather than spitting it into a bucket.

6. *Make a Note—Written or Mental:* If you are at a serious tasting, most people will be making written notes on the

wines they are tasting. If you are at a dinner table or friend's living room, you should just make a permanent mental note of a wine you really like.

Buying Wine in a Restaurant

The more you learn about wine, the more painfully aware you become of the prices of wine in restaurants. If you enjoy going to restaurants and want to enjoy wine when you are there, consider the following:

Food Is Often Marked Up More Than Wine

Good restaurants usually mark up food 2fi times, in other words, a $20 entree would cost the restaurant $8. While some restaurants mark up wine as much, most charge around double their cost for midrange wines.

It is true that the restaurant adds expertise and convenience to the raw ingredients of your entree. Insist on the same with your wine—proper temperature, sparkling clean and appropriate glassware, and proper, attentive service.

You Can Send It Back

. . . within reason. If a wine has gone bad, has suffered from a spoiled cork (commonly referred to as "corked"), has turned sour, or smells rotten, any restaurant should gladly take it back. If a wine steward or waiter has enthusiastically recommended a wine and you don't like it, you should be allowed to return it. But, if you simply don't like a wine, step back a bit. Do others at your table agree? Have you tasted it without food? If so, taste it with a well-chewed piece of bread in your mouth. Wine is meant to be tasted with food. Might it need to breathe? If you aren't sure, ask the waiter to pour some wine into a glass, and let it breathe for a few minutes. If you still just don't like it, a good restaurant will probably try to keep you happy. It is best not to make a habit of this practice. By the way, most wines sent back in restaurants go back to the supplier, thus relieving the restaurant of the cost. The exception to this is older wine.

Let's say you order a twenty-year-old Bordeaux. This wine may have been in the restaurant's cellar for fifteen years. For $100 a bottle you have a right to expect good, solid wine. However, can you send it back if, while

showing no flaws, it fails to provide the
expected religious experience? Probably, but
you should consider that the price of
older wine often reflects its scarcity
rather than its intrinsic value. You
pay a premium for the opportunity
to enjoy wine on your twentieth
anniversary from, say, the year of your
marriage. So, be thoughtful about returning
such wines—the restaurant will probably
have to eat the cost of the bottle (which,
when they bought it, might have been surprisingly little money).

How Wines Go Bad

Red wine. If the fruit vanishes and the
color fades, it's too old. A brown color or a
vinegary taste indicates improper storage.

White wine. If it's brown colored or tastes burnt, it is too old or was improperly stored.

Either wine can be "corked"—when the cork is partially dissolved into the wine by biological activity.

Sparkling wine. No fizz indicates improper storage or a wine that is too old.

Wine by the Glass Is Usually a Rip-Off

The markup on bottles of wine is far less than the markup on mixed drinks. Many customers now order a glass of wine in place of that initial cocktail, so smart restaurant operators make sure that they make the same money on that drink and mark up wine by the glass accordingly. A better value is premium

wine by the glass, a category in which the markup is more in line with the wine program than with the martini program. These premium wines by the glass are a convenient service for those who can't agree on a bottle or don't want to drink that much.

Know the Price Structure

In a retail store, you can calculate the price of wines very easily. In most cases the wine costs about 50 percent over wholesale. After a few shopping trips, you will know what the most commonly sold wines in your area cost on the wholesale level.

Good restaurants often mark up more expensive wines at a lower percentage than their inexpensive choices. This encourages customers to "trade up" for better value.

In a good restaurant with fairly priced food and wine, wine as good as the food will cost about twice the price of the average entree.

Enjoying Wine with Your Dinner

Just as at home, in a restaurant you have some control over the enjoyment of your wine. Is this white too cold? Let it warm up on the table and in the glass, and taste the hidden flavors as they emerge. Is the red too warm? Your server should cool it for you in ice water for five minutes or so. Your server should be pouring it for you—in proper glass-ware, never more than half full—though it's okay to pour it yourself.

The Wine Ritual

You ordered the wine, and you are shown the label. Is it the right year? If you ordered a "reserve," make sure it is not a lesser bottling from the same producer. So far, so good. Tell the server to keep the cork, unless you collect corks; it is of no use to you once you have verified that it hasn't rotted during its years in the bottle. Do taste the wine while the server is there. Any problem should be addressed immediately. Your server should then pour wine for everyone at the table.

Tipping on Wine

Many people treat tipping on wine as a separate issue. There's no need to. Just tip on the whole bill, with maybe an extra $5-10 to the wine steward (or server) for an especially enjoyable recommendation.

An alternative tipping strategy is to tip 20 percent on your food and 10–15 percent on your restaurant wine purchases.

CHAPTER 2

Wine and Food

Food and wine have always been a great combination at the dinner table. Meals featuring wine have come to symbolize good times. Here is a partial list of reasons, past and present, why people enjoy wine and food together:

1. Few other beverage options existed centuries ago.
2. Pure drinking water has not always been widely available.
3. Wine assists in the digestion of food.

4. Certain wines are so delicious with certain foods that they enhance each other and your enjoyment.
5. When a meal is served as a celebration or holiday feast, the alcohol in wine raises everyone's spirits.
6. Wine enhances the intimacy of a romantic meal.

You can probably think of other good reasons for matching wine with food. Of course, just as you can enjoy food without wine, you can enjoy many wines without food. Sweet wines, wines naturally low in alcohol, and low-acid wines are easy to enjoy alone. Rich, chewy wines may be too much flavor for your taste at the dinner table.

Matching Food and Wine

Many people are familiar with
the old, well-established rule of
food/wine pairing— "White wine
with fish, red wine with meat."
While this rule is not as valid as it
once was (we'll show you why), the reasoning
behind it is sound and deserves examination.

Think of a nice, fresh fillet of sole, neatly
grilled. Most of us who enjoy fish would welcome a squeeze of fresh lemon on it. Why?
The acid in the lemon "cuts" the intrinsic
fish flavor without overpowering it. Thus
white wine, with its more apparent acidity
and less powerful flavors, would be more
appropriate for sole than red wine.

Imagine a roast beef with delicious gravy
made from onions and pan drippings. The

assertive flavor of the gravy matches in magnitude the flavor of the beef, as would a rich red wine. Just as onion gravy would overwhelm the fillet of sole, so would most red wines. And just as a squeeze of lemon would be lost on the roast beef, so too would most white wines. If only it were that simple.

The increasing complexity of food is the most troublesome for matching wine with food. Here are some guidelines (not rules) that will help.

Don't dwell on color. There are enough other factors to consider; the color will take care of itself. For instance, chicken dishes can be prepared to match well with any wine, depending on the ingredients. Lighter reds and strong whites can survive most food pairings.

Match strengths. Powerfully flavored dishes require wines of equal fortitude. Example: Herb-crusted leg of lamb or garlicky ratatouille match well with a strongly flavored wine, usually red.

Delicate dishes need delicate wine. Example: Simply prepared white fish (like sole) need a gentle wine, usually white.

Opposites attract. The spicy cuisine of the Pacific Rim needs a light, sweet wine to extinguish the fire. Rich cream or butter sauces are well matched with an acidic, "cutting wine."

You don't need to match!

So you love sole and you love Cabernet Sauvignon . . . Fine! Have them together. A sip of water and a nibble of bread will smooth the transition from one to the other.

Regional affinity. In Europe it is a truism that regional cooking goes best with the local wine.

Simple wine with complex food. Pair this food with a varietal not inclined to great complexity—Pinot Blanc (among whites) and Merlot (among reds) come to mind.

Complex wine with simple food. The best way to showcase a fabulously complex (and expensive) wine is to pair it with a simple, yet delicious, background dish. Examples: A super-premium Cabernet Sauvignon with plain grilled steak or a great white Burgundy (Chardonnay) with plain broiled fish.

Match price. A $50 Chianti would be wasted on a pizza, but a carefully prepared dinner deserves an equally special wine.

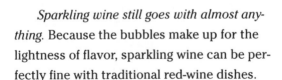

Sparkling wine still goes with almost anything. Because the bubbles make up for the lightness of flavor, sparkling wine can be perfectly fine with traditional red-wine dishes.

And so does rosé. Wine snobs are quick to dismiss rosé. If it tastes good, drink it. Although it is not really "right" with any food, it isn't really "wrong" either, unless, of course, you don't like rosé.

Match wine to the occasion. The above-mentioned rosé is frequently mentioned as a "picnic wine." Informal gatherings call for informal wine.

Serving red wine with fish. As long as the acid level is high and the tannins are barely noticeable, red wine is fine with most seafood. Here are some suggestions:

- Simple Chianti or other Sangiovese-based Italian wine
- Certain Pinot Noirs—Côte de Beaune, Chalonnais, Oregon, lighter California
- Beaujolais or other Gamay-based wines
- Lighter versions of Merlot (or Merlot blends)—Saint-Emilion (Bordeaux) is especially good.
- Rioja, from Spain—Though not high in acid, these Tempranillo-based wines are versatile and inoffensive.

White wine with beef. Certain whites are big enough to stand up to charred sirloin and other beef dishes. Consider high-alcohol and well-oaked California or Australian Chardonnay. Viognier-based whites are

Wine and Food Matches

Red Meat Dishes

Chili con carne Beaujolais (an easy-drinking red); Zinfandel (a red to stand up to your chili)

Grilled steak Cabernet Sauvignon (an ultimate match); Shiraz/Syrah (a good choice at a better price)

Hamburger Any red wine you like that is inexpensive

Roast beef Pinot Noir and Merlot (softer reds than for your grilled steak). If you are wild about Cabernet Sauvignon, then have a Cabernet from Bordeaux.

Steak au poivre (Steak with black peppercorn sauce) BIG REDS!—Zinfandel from California and Rhône reds are perfect

Tenderloin Same as for roast beef: Pinot Noir and Merlot are the best choices.

Other Meat Dishes

Chicken (roasted) Almost any wine you like—this is a very versatile dish.

Chicken (highly seasoned) Chenin Blanc and Riesling

Duck/Goose/Game birds Pinot Blanc or Viognier (whites); Pinot Noir or Merlot (reds)

Ham Rosé; California Pinot Noir; demi-sec Vouvray; Gewürztraminer

Lamb (simple) Cabernet (especially from Bordeaux); Rioja red from Spain

up for the challenge as well. This offbeat varietal can be one of the most pleasant surprises of the wine world.

Serve cheaper wines with cheese. The fat in cheese makes wine taste better. This makes cheese an important ingredient at receptions at which large quantities of inexpensive wine are served.

Fruit and wine don't match. Most fruits are acidic, and so are most wines. Fruit acids can throw a good wine out of balance.

Wine and chocolate don't match. And they never will, although it's fun to try!

White Wine with Red Meat (Anti-Match #1)

So you all want steak and white wine . . . a sommelier's nightmare? Not really. There are some

Wine and Food Matches

Other Meat Dishes

Lamb (with herbs and garlic) The herbs and garlic are going to cut into your ability to taste the wine. Try a big red (a steak au poivre wine). And go easy on the garlic.

Pork An Italian or Spanish red; any white you like

Sausage Gewürztraminer or an ordinary red

Turkey Rosé; any white you like; a very light red

Veal California Chardonnay is perfect

Venison (deer) A big red wine—Cabernet, Nebbiolo, Syrah, or Zinfandel will do

Seafood Dishes

Anything with a cream sauce White Burgundy (clean, crisp Chardonnay)

Lobster Champagne; dry Riesling; white Burgundy

Oysters Muscadet, a French white, is ideal with oysters; Chablis (dry French Chardonnay) or Champagne

Salmon Sauvignon Blanc

Shrimp Light and dry white wine

Swordfish White wine

Tuna Versatile like chicken; anything but a big red is okay. A light red is probably the ideal match.

White fish (sole, etc.) Sauvignon Blanc, light Chardonnay

big, strapping Chardonnays from California's Sonoma and Napa regions that could hold their own with just about any dish and. The secret is wood, an important component of any big California Chardonnay. Ripe Chardonnay fruit, high alcohol, and a glycerine-charged body benefit from new-oak aging, which seems to unify these powerful components while adding further complexity. Australian and Santa Barbara Chardonnays also qualify but are likely to show more fruit than wood. Big French Chardonnays from the Côte de Beaune are a possibility, but their higher acidity and more subtle charms may be lost on red meat.

If you are less interested in the wine than the food, any subtle

Wine and Food Matches

Pasta Dishes

Red sauce Chianti or other Sangiovese-based red

Vegetables Pinot Grigio; light red

White sauce Pinot Grigio

Indian & Asian Cuisine

These food cultures developed without wine, except for rice wine (saké). Beer is often a better match. German Riesling and inexpensive sparkling wines are your best wine choices, or Beaujolais if your wine has to be red.

Pizza

Rioja red, Italian red, Canadian red, any red—unless you like white, then any white. After all, pizza is the no-fuss food. Don't spend a lot of money on this match.

Vegetarian Dishes

Red beans and darker starches and vegetables go with red wine. Lighter and greener foods go better with white wine. Petite Sirah is quite good with hearty vegetable dishes like vegetarian chili.

white wine can be served, but the wine's flavors won't be easily noticed.

Red Wine with Fish (Anti-Match #2)

This is a hip way to break the rules, especially with something like a tuna or swordfish steak. Look for high-acid, low-tannin wines—Italian reds tend to be versatile, as are Pinot Noirs from Oregon and Burgundy. California Pinot Noir is probably going to be too fruity. Rioja may be okay with fish. French Saint-Emilion, in which Merlot usually predominates, is a light take on a fruity grape and a decent match with fish. European wines are crafted to be food friendly. This is good to remember when you are trying to make an unorthodox food/wine match like fish with red wine.

Wine and Food Matches

Snacks

Bread Everything goes with bread.

Caviar Champagne and money; Vodka and money

Cheese: rich and creamy (i.e., Brie, Camembert) Sauternes or an off-dry Riesling

Cheese: goat, and feta A Spanish or Italian red, although most wines, red or white, go okay.

Cheese: other Whatever wine you want. Cheese makes cheap wine taste better!

Fruit Not a good match with wine. Grapes especially are very bad with wine.

Pâté Gewürztraminer or light red

Rich pâté (i.e., foie gras) Sauternes or an off-dry Riesling

Salty snacks Something cheap. Remember to quench your thirst with water, not wine.

If you end up with a red that is powerfully flavored, you are going to end up missing most of the fish's flavor. If you have a wine that is too strong for your fish or any meal, put it aside and drink it after you finish your food. The better the fish, the more you'll want to preserve the food experience.

As a general rule, fish that is grilled takes on a charred flavor that makes it more compatible with red wines than white. It stands to reason that the fish we usually grill are quite flavorful to begin with—salmon, tuna, swordfish, and shark.

Letting Wine Breathe

What is breathing? It is exposing wine to air, aerating it. White wines don't seem to react right away to oxygen, so when we talk about letting a wine breathe, we are talking about a red wine.

Practically all wine is crafted in a way that causes it to evolve over time. If this were

not the case, then we'd be buying and
drinking month-old wine like we buy month-
old beer (if we're lucky). A large part of the
evolution is the mellowing of the wine.
Tannins and acids are the components that
most need to mellow.
Without sufficient expo-
sure to oxygen, wines
can taste harsh.
Eventually, as the tan-
nins and/or acids
fade a bit, the fruit
begins to exert itself

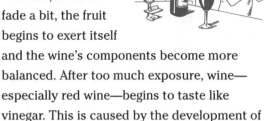

and the wine's components become more
balanced. After too much exposure, wine—
especially red wine—begins to taste like
vinegar. This is caused by the development of
acetic acid.

A Zinfandel, Cabernet Sauvignon, Shiraz/Syrah, or Nebbiolo may need to breathe for an hour or more, depending on how the wine was made and how mature it is. Equally important are the personal tastes of the people who will be drinking the wine. Some people like to taste wines right out of the bottle and experience the evolution over time. A Beaujolais Nouveau doesn't need to breathe much. This makes sense, as it is crafted not to evolve but to be drunk just weeks after harvest.

Generally speaking, all red wines taste better ten minutes after you open the bottle and pour it into the glass. Just taking the cork out and leaving the wine in the bottle is ineffective, since so little of the wine is exposed to air. Let your wine breathe in a glass. Wines that are still before their peak when the cork is removed may taste much better after half an hour or more in a glass.

Letting your wine breathe doesn't have to be a controlled scientific experiment. It is interesting merely to observe how bad some good wines may taste when you first open the bottle. Just keep in mind that a red wine will probably be better (and unlikely to be worse) after ten minutes of aeration. A white wine may also benefit from some air and is unlikely to taste worse. Some wines actually taste better the next day. We've had some $6 bottles of red wine that tasted like $12 bottles the next day. It's important to note that these wines were in a recorked bottle and not left out for a day in a wine glass.

If you ever have an expensive bottle of wine fifteen or more years old, you don't want to give it much air time. These wines can change drastically literally from minute to minute. Because a lot of the mellowing has already been done by sitting in the bottle for years, these wines may run out of gas an hour after the bottle is opened. Don't bother saving part of an old wine for the next day unless you want to experiment: It will probably be dead.

CHAPTER 3

Varietal Wines, Grape by Grape

Wine is made from grapes unless otherwise labeled as pear wine, blueberry wine, etc. Grape varieties vary greatly in color and character as well as in winemaking potential. Although there are many species of grapes, most of the world's wines come from the *Vitis vinifera* family, the classic European grape family whose vines were first brought to America prior to the American Revolution. Early American wine came from the *Vitis labrusca* and the Ohio River Valley's *Vitis riparia* species of grapes. The Scuppernong grape, thought to be the first native grape American settlers tried to turn into wine, is a member of the *Vitis rotundifolia* species of grape.

Vitis labrusca's most famous family member is the Concord grape. Today, it is not given much serious consideration by the wine world. However, decent wine can be coaxed out of it. Generally, these grapes are used to make grape juice and grape jelly rather than wine.

The biggest contribution *labrusca* grapes have made to the wine world is to be an organ donor for disease-prone *vinifera* vines. Many of the *vinifera* vines around the world today are grafted onto *labrusca* roots.

The *vinifera* family of grapes, which come in red, black, and green varieties, is used to make the vast majority of the world's wine. It is believed that these grapes originated in Asia Minor. The wine world has a term for a small subset of the *vinifera* family that produces the world's top wines: noble grapes. Cabernet Sauvignon, Pinot Noir, Merlot, Syrah, Sangiovese, and Nebbiolo are the noble red grapes. Riesling,

Varietal Correctness

Wine grapes have certain signature characteristics. Body, flavors, and textures are the most obvious. If you buy an inferior wine made from inferior grapes, you will not be able to recognize the grape because its signature characteristics are missing. When you drink the following wines, have your tongue and nose on the lookout for their signature flavor characteristics:

Cabernet Sauvignon: Cassis, mint, bell peppers
Merlot: Blueberries, plums, tar
Pinot Noir: Cherries, fresh ground coffee, soil, raspberries
Zinfandel: Berries, black pepper
Gamay: Strawberries
Chardonnay: Apples, pears, pineapples, bananas
Gewürztraminer: Lychee nuts, spices
Semillon: Figs

Chardonnay, and Sauvignon Blanc are the noble white grapes.

Varietal wines—those labeled and sold according to the grape variety from which they are made—must meet government-determined minimum varietal percentages. This is the minimum percentage of a wine that must be made from the grape variety under which it is being sold. Although your bottle says Chardonnay, there is a very good chance that juices from other grapes are also in the bottle. These minor-percentage grapes are not usually credited on the bottle.

Cabernet Sauvignon

Main growing regions: Bordeaux (France), Australia, California, Washington State, Chile, and Tuscany (Italy)

Aromas and flavors: Black currants, green peppers, chocolate, and spice

Acidity: Moderate

Tannin: Moderate to prominent

Body: Moderate to full

Major mixing partners: Sangiovese (Tuscany), Merlot (Bordeaux), Shiraz (Australia)

Cabernet Sauvignon first became noteworthy as a grape variety in Bordeaux in the late 1700s. Today this variety is at or near the top of every connoisseur's great red varietal list. Appearing either alone or in combination with other varietals, Cabernet Sauvignon generally makes rich, tannic wines capable of commanding high prices. Typical tasting comments on young Cabernets usually praise the black currant, bell pepper, chocolate, and spice flavors. With its forthright fruit flavors, Cabernet Sauvignon benefits from contact with new oak, which lends balance and further complexity.

There are several exquisite versions of Cabernet Sauvignon from California, particularly from the Napa Valley, that are not blended with other grapes. One of the most famous and expensive of these is Heitz Cellar "Martha's Vineyard" Cabernet Sauvignon.

As a blending grape, Cabernet Sauvignon successfully shares a bottle with Syrah (Shiraz) in wines from Australia, and with Sangiovese in "super-Tuscan" wines from Italy. In Bordeaux, Cabernet Sauvignon is usually blended with a combination of Merlot, Cabernet Franc (a relative), Malbec, and Petite Verdot. United States law requires a

minimum of 75 percent of a particular grape
variety in order to qualify for varietal labeling.
The California wine industry coined the term

Good Cabernet Sauvignon

1. Santa Rita Cabernet Sauvignon (Chile) $6
2. Monterey Vineyard Cabernet Sauvignon
   (Monterey, California) $9
3. Terra Rosa Cabernet Sauvignon (California) $12
4. Liberty School Cabernet Sauvignon (California) . .$15
5. Franciscan Cabernet Sauvignon (Napa, California) $24
6. Jordan Cabernet Sauvignon
   (Alexander Valley, California) $35
7. Pride Mountain Cabernet Sauvignon
   (Napa, California) $45
8. B. R. Cohn "Olive Hill" Cabernet Sauvignon
   (Sonoma, California) $45
9. Beringer Private Reserve Cabernet Sauvignon
   (Napa, California) $85
10. Spottswoode Cabernet Sauvignon
    (Napa, California) $100

"Meritage" in order to distinguish these fine blended wines from ordinary table wines.

In any wine shop one might find varietal Cabernet Sauvignon from Chile, Australia, Californina, Washington State, Italy, Spain, or France. Expensive as great Cabernet Sauvignon can be, the bargains are out there. Look for varietal wines from the south of France (labeled *vin du pays d'oc* or Languedoc) and also from Chile. The Cabernet/Shiraz blends from Australia are often excellent values.

There are a handful of ultra-expensive, reserve Cabernet Sauvignons and Meritage wines from Napa Valley, California: Beaulieu Vineyard "Georges Latour Private Reserve," Caymus "Special Select," Far Niente, Opus One, Niebaum-Coppola "Rubican," and Stag's Leap "Cask 23." From Penfold's in Australia comes the noteworthy Cabernet Sauvignon Bin 707. Winemakers Miguel Torres and Jean Leon are producing high-quality Cabernet Sauvignon in the Penedés region of north-eastern Spain, and the iconoclastic wine-maker Gaston Hochar planted Cabernet Sauvignon in Lebanon, where it is blended with Syrah and Cinsault in his famous Château Musar wine.

It is in the Bordeaux subregions of Médoc and Graxas where the most elegant, age-worthy, and expensive Cabernet Sauvignon-based wines are produced. Two of the top–rated Bordeaux châteaux, Château Mouton-Rothschild and Château Latour, rely on Cabernet Sauvignon for 70 percent of their blends. These and other highly rated

WELL I GUESS IT'S ABOUT READY.

Bordeaux châteaux produce wines that can age well for many decades and command hundreds of dollars for a bottle from a great year.

The assertive flavors of Cabernet Sauvignon—young or old—match nicely with lamb, beef, and other red meat dishes. Young Cabernet Sauvignon is especially well paired with meats from the grill because the youthful fruit flavors are a perfect counterpoint to the pleasantly bitter scorch imparted by the open fire.

So what does Cabernet Sauvignon do for an encore? Some of the finest rosé wines in the world are made from this wonder grape. Look for Simi Rosé of Cabernet Sauvignon from the Sonoma Valley.

Pinot Noir

Main growing regions:	Burgundy (France), California, and Oregon
Aromas and Flavors:	Cherries, raspberries, and smoke
Acidity:	Moderate to high
Tannin:	Low to moderate
Body:	Light to medium
Major mixing partners:	None

If it were not so difficult to grow, Pinot Noir would enjoy a reputation for greatness equal to that of Cabernet Sauvignon. It is the noble red grape of France's Burgundy region where, under ideal conditions, it yields ruby-colored wines whose velvety richness has seduced wine lovers for centuries.

Except for a few pockets (Santa Barbara and Carneros, to name two), Pinot Noir seems to be most at home in the U.S. up north in Oregon, where the long, cool growing season allows the Pinot Noir fruit flavors to develop slowly. Pinot Noir ripened quickly on the hot California valley floors tends to be flat and uninteresting.

Less pigmented than most red grapes, Pinot Noir has a brick-orange cast rather than a deep purple color. At its best, Pinot Noir is low in tannin and high in glycerine (hence, the "velvet"), and has a lively acidic backbone that gives length and focus to the typical Pinot Noir flavors of raspberries, cherries, and smoke. Such structure makes Pinot Noir a highly versatile food wine.

Full-bodied red Burgundy from the Côte de Nuits subregion is made entirely from Pinot Noir and is a classic accompaniment to beef roasts. The lighter red Burgundies from the Côte de Beaune are perfect with game birds such as pheasant and partridge. The

Pinot Noirs from Oregon can be very
Burgundian in structure and range from a
light Côte de Beaune style to a richer Côte de

Good Pinot Noir

1. Fireskeed Pinot Noir (Oregon) $10
2. Villa Mt. Eden Pinot Noir (California) $12
3. Elk Cove Pinot Noir (Oregon) $14
4. Louis Latour Bourgogne Pinot Noir
   (Burgundy, France) $15
5. Estancia Pinot Noir (Monterey, California) $16
6. Sterling "Winery Lake" Pinot Noir
   (Napa, California) $18
7. Eyrie Vineyards Pinot Noir Reserve (Oregon) $22
8. Steele Pinot Noir (Carneros, California) $23
9. Joseph Drouhin Mercurey (Burgundy, France) ... $23
10. Gary Farrell (Sonoma) $24
11. Byron Pinot Noir (Santa Barbara, California) $25
12. Hanzell Pinot Noir (Sonoma, California) $28
13. Truchard Vineyards Pinot Noir (Napa, California) $29
14. Domaine Drouhin Pinot Noir (Oregon) $40
15. Louis Latour Gevrey-Chambertin
    (Burgundy, France) $50

Nuits style; they match with food accordingly. The light, clean acidity and modest tannin of typical Pinot Noir makes it suitable with all but the lightest of seafood dishes. Open one of the jammy Californian interpretations of Pinot Noir—from Santa Barbara, Carneros, or the Russian River Valley in Sonoma—in place of Merlot. You'll find that these generously fruity and mildly acidic wines might be more enjoyable.

Perhaps the best use of Pinot Noir grapes in California is as the main component in brut rosé–style, Blanc de Noirs sparkling wines. Several of the great French Champagne houses, in order to meet growing worldwide demand, opened shop in California. Here they found that Pinot Noir, a vital component of Champagne in France, grows to full ripeness in the California sunshine. More ripeness means more color in the skin and more fruit flavors as well.

Decent Pinot Noir is never cheap. A good way to get to know this grape is by trying varietal-labeled Pinot Noir from the big, reputable Burgundy (Bourgogne as it's known in France) houses. These will usually be labeled "Bourgogne Pinot Noir." The Chalonnais subregion of Burgundy offers two inexpensive and enjoyable Pinot Noir–based wines: Givry and Mercurey.

Most Oregonian interpretations of Pinot Noir are closer in style to their Burgundian brethren than they are to their Californian neighbors. Ask a reliable wine merchant for his or her suggestions for a varietally correct

I RECKON I'LL HAVE A SHOT OF PINOT NOIR—STRAIGHT

(yet affordable) Pinot Noir. Oregon Pinot bargains are definitely available.

Merlot

Main growing regions:	Bordeaux (France), California, Washington State, Australia, Chile
Aromas and flavors:	Plums, blueberries, and cherries
Acidity:	Low
Tannin:	Low to moderate
Body:	Medium
Major mixing partner:	Cabernet Sauvignon (Bordeaux)

Just as Cabernet Sauvignon gained recognition in the Médoc subregion of Bordeaux in the late 1700s, so too did Merlot become prominent in the cooler Bordeaux subregions of Pomerol and Saint-Emilion. Merlot grows much better in cooler climates than does Cabernet Sauvignon, although not too cool;

Merlot has yet to gain a foothold in chilly
Oregon where Pinot Noir is king.

Merlot is a distant relative
of Cabernet Sauvignon. The
biggest difference is that the
skin of the Merlot grape is
thinner than that of Cabernet
Sauvignon; therefore, Merlot is
the earlier ripening and less

tannic of the two. Merlot has a reputation for
making soft, round, and drinkable wines with
low acidity and generous fruit flavors of plum,
blueberry, and cherry along with a pleasantly
chalky texture.

Until recently, Merlot's primary role had
been in blends with Cabernet Sauvignon. In
the past few years, however, the Merlot grape
has made the transition from being an assis-

tant to Cabernet Sauvignon in blended wines to being a star in its own right.

California had only a few acres of this variety planted since the mid-1970s. When red wine came back into vogue, it seems that every winery so capable planted additional Merlot acreage as soon as possible, and the resulting wines were often disappointing. Grapes from very young vines growing in marginal areas are usually pressed too hard (the better to extract every drop of pricey nectar, with the inevitable concentration of unwanted tannin). It is now almost impossible to buy delicious, varietally correct Merlot for under $8.

In the meantime, the best bargains in varietal Merlot are the Languedoc and *vin de pays* wines of

France. South America (Chile and Argentina) produces good, affordable Merlot as well.

What are the characteristics of a good Merlot? Look for rich, plum-like fruit, almost jammy in its concentration, and low levels of acid and tannin. Merlot does not get particularly complex; yet because of its soft tannin and gentle acidity profile, its pleasing fruit flavors are more accessible than those in sturdier reds.

The soft tannin also makes Merlot an enjoyable match with a broad variety of foods. Even seafood, especially from the grill, can be a lovely pairing with Merlot's unobtrusive flavors. Its somewhat bland personality allows Merlot to fit nicely with all types of well-seasoned ethnic dishes.

Because it is easy to drink in comparison to other red-wine varieties, Merlot has become many red-wine neophytes' wine of choice. This has caused a tremendous "Merlot boom." Like many fads, this one will cost you if you want to be a part of it. Comparable (in quality, not taste) red wines made from different grapes often cost less.

In response to the Merlot boom, the wine market now offers us an enormous selection of choices from around the world, many of which did not exist a decade ago. Here is a list of recommended Merlots at various prices.

The Merlot Spectrum

Group 1 Under $10: Cheap, enjoyable, and the label says Merlot. These wines would be difficult to recognize as Merlot if tasted blind, but they nonetheless taste pretty good. Just about every winemaking country is represented in Group 1, making for

The Merlot Spectrum

Group 1 Recommendations

1. Marcus James (Brazil) $5
2. Georges Duboeuf Domaine de Bordeneuve
   (France) $5
3. Lirico (Veneto, Italy) $6
4. Santa Rita (Chile) $6
5. Dulong (France) $6
6. Domaine Caton (France) . . . .$7/1.0 liters
7. Dunnewood (California) $7
8. Rene Barbier Mediterranean Select Merlot
   (Penedés, Spain) $8
9. Emerald Bay (California) $8
10. Hardy's "Nottage Hill" (South Australia) $9
11. Concha y Toro (Chile) . . . .$9/1.5 liters
12. Mezzacorona (Italy) $9
13. Fortant de France Kosher Merlot (France) $9

Group 2 Recommendations

1. Forest Glen (California) $10
2. Swartland (South Africa) $10
3. Christian Moueix Merlot (Bordeaux, France) $12
4. Blackstone (California) $12
5. Covey Run (Washington) $13
6. Columbia Crest (Washington) $14
7. Hyatt (Washington) $15

some interesting (and affordable!) comparison taste testing.

Group 2 $10–15: The threshold of varietal correctness. Once you pass through the $10 barrier, you can find Merlot that is easily identifiable as such. You will notice a fair amount of Washington State wines. Merlot is an early ripening grape and thus does well in the cooler growing regions of Washington.

Group 3 $16–19: Fruity, full-bodied, and complex. This price range is where truly delicious Merlot begins. At these prices, winemakers can afford to use higher quality grapes and the more expensive winemaking techniques such as proper cooperage (barrels) and gentle pressing. As a result these wines are fruity, full-bodied, and complex. Most importantly, they have the velvety texture that is the signature of good Merlot.

Group 4 $21–29: Hand-crafted master-pieces. In this price range we escape the dollar-driven feeding frenzy and enter more exclusive territory—sort of like leaving the department store for a pricey boutique.

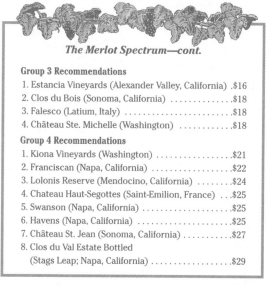

The Merlot Spectrum—cont.

Group 3 Recommendations
1. Estancia Vineyards (Alexander Valley, California) .$16
2. Clos du Bois (Sonoma, California) $18
3. Falesco (Latium, Italy) $18
4. Château Ste. Michelle (Washington) $18

Group 4 Recommendations
1. Kiona Vineyards (Washington) $21
2. Franciscan (Napa, California) $22
3. Lolonis Reserve (Mendocino, California) $24
4. Chateau Haut-Segottes (Saint-Emilion, France) . . .$25
5. Swanson (Napa, California) $25
6. Havens (Napa, California) $25
7. Château St. Jean (Sonoma, California) $27
8. Clos du Val Estate Bottled
    (Stags Leap; Napa, California) $29

Notice the French wine in this price range; Saint-Emilion is a subregion of the Bordeaux region. Like most fine French wines, it seems light bodied in comparison to its California counterparts. No one disputes its subtlety and finesse.

Group 5 $30–70: Power Merlot—you have to know somebody to buy these. Among the professional elite in many vocations—the legal profession comes to mind—the ability to procure certain rare wines is regarded as manly. Accordingly, the feeding frenzy for these tightly allocated wines is every bit as rabid as that for lower-priced Merlots. Fortunately, this foolishness is generally confined to the wines of California, and the four Pomerol wines on this list are more widely available.

If you wish to continue your journey up-
market, you must leave California. With the
exception of the one "super Tuscan" from
Italy, Pomerol (France) is the promised land.

The Merlot Spectrum—cont.

Group 5 Recommendations

1. Sullivan (Napa, California) $30
2. Château Clos L'Eglise (Pomerol, France) $30
3. Stonestreet (Sonoma, California) $30
4. Justin (Paso Robles, California) $32
5. Kenwood "Jack London" (Sonoma, California) . . .$32
6. Château Beauregard (Pomerol, France) $36
7. Duckhorn (Napa, California) $45
8. Pride Mountain (Napa, California) $45
9. Avignonese (Tuscany, Italy) $48
10. Château Gazin (Pomerol, France) $50
11. Château L'Eglise Clinet (Pomerol, France) $50
12. Matanzas Creek (Sonoma, California) $58
13. Château La Pointe (Pomerol, France) $60
14. Newton "Unfiltered" (Napa, California) $60
15. Duckhorn "Three Palms" (Napa, California) $70

- 1990 Fattoria di Ama Merlot
  "Apparita" (Tuscany) $100
- 1990 Château Trotanoy
  (Pomerol) $170
- 1990 Vieux-Château-Certan
  (Pomerol) $170
- 1990 Château Certan-de-May
  (Pomerol) $170

Still not satisfied? Perhaps Château Petrus is the wine for you. The 1990 Petrus now sells for over $1,000/bottle in some places. A prisoner of its own popularity, Château Petrus is generally regarded as too expensive to drink at any point in its life.

Rarer yet is Château Le Pin from Pomerol. Only 500 cases (6,000 bottles)

of the 1994 were produced, as opposed to
3,200 cases of Petrus, and it goes for $400 per
bottle.

Syrah/Shiraz

Main growing regions:	Rhône (France), Australia, and California
Aromas and flavors:	Prunes, spices, and berries
Acidity:	Low to moderate
Tannin:	Moderate to prominent
Body:	Medium
Major mixing partners:	Grenache (Rhône) and Cabernet Sauvignon (Australia)

The Syrah grape, known as Shiraz in Australia
and South Africa, is a noble grape variety held
in high esteem by many red-wine lovers. The
great and ageworthy wines of the northern
Rhône—Hermitage, Côte Rôtie, St. Joseph,
and Cornas—are produced from unblended
Syrah. The finest wine produced in Australia

is Penfold's Hermitage, another example of unblended Shiraz at its finest. Australian varietal Shiraz is as common as Shiraz/Cabernet Sauvignon blends; the latter are remarkable bargains.

The Syrah grape is believed by some to have originated in ancient Persia. Syrah seems to have brought along a whiff of exotic Eastern spices in its travels to France, Australia, and California. The subtle spiciness in its aroma, often a combination of cinnamon, rose petals, and orange rind, complements flavors of raspberry and black pepper. These qualities require bottle aging in order to emerge; youthful Syrah wines usually exhibit more power than finesse. Well-aged Syrah is rare in the wine market, but experience shows that mature Syrah is well worth the wait.

California got a late start with this variety. It seems that another grape from the Rhône valley, perhaps the Duriff grape, was transplanted by accident rather than Syrah.

Good Syrah (Shiraz)

1. B & G Syrah (France) $8
2. Thomas Hardy Shiraz/Cabernet (Australia) $9
3. McGuigan's "Black Label" (Australia) $10
4. Rosemount Shiraz (Australia) $13
5. Leasingham Estate Shiraz (Australia) $18
6. Qupe Syrah (Santa Barbara, California) $20
7. Château Reynella (Australia) $24
8. Selby Syrah (Sonoma, California) $25
9. Guigal Côte Rôtie, Côtes Brune et Blonde
   (Rhône, France) $35
10. J. Vidal Fleury Hermitage Rouge (Rhône, France) .$37

Today that grape is known in California as Petite Sirah, and the true Syrah is a relatively recent arrival in California. Some California Syrahs are quite good, but Australia, with a hundred-year head start, is the source for bargains in Shiraz.

In general, the French version is higher in acid and better with food than the Australian version, which shows more fruit. This is because of the difference in climate. The warmer weather of Australia leads to a more thorough ripening of the grape, which in turn leads to more fruitiness and a lower acidity in the wine. Whereas the French Syrahs tend to display raspberry-like fruit aromas, the Australian versions are often more suggestive of raisins.

Zinfandel

Main growing region: California

Aromas and flavors: Blackberry jam and black pepper

Acidity: Low to moderate

Tannin: Moderate, can be substantial in some versions

Body: Medium to full

Major mixing partners: Often blended, but rarely credited (California)

This popular grape, of unclear origin (probably an obscure European variety) showed up in California in the mid-1800s and has been growing like a weed since then. No other *vinifera* grape so thrives on California heat and sunshine. Unfortunately, the evolution of Zinfandel got sidetracked by the creation of the wildly popular rosé, white Zinfandel in the early 1970s.

As a result of this, wine lists must now use the retronym "red Zinfandel" to indicate the varietal in its original form. Zinfandel is as versatile as it is prolific, capable of a broad range of styles. In addition to white Zinfandel, which is actually a rosé, Zinfandel can range from a light, Beaujolais-like quaff to late-harvest brutes that practically ooze pepper and jammy fruit. Although $5 won't get you a bottle of Zinfandel, $10 bottles do exist and they are often quite good.

If you suffer sticker shock from a reserve Cabernet Sauvignon or Meritage, opt for an estate-bottled "old vines" Zinfandel ($15–20). Its complexity, power, and balance should impress you for the money. These wines are especially well matched with roasted lamb and other Mediterranean dishes, even hearty vegetable dishes. Zinfandel stands up well to garlic and powerful seasonings. These buxom, fruity wines are great alone or with a wine-friendly snack of cheese and crackers.

Good (Red) Zinfandel

1. Talus (California) $10
2. Ravenswood (Sonoma, California) $12
3. Mazzocco (Sonoma, California) $15
4. Rodney Strong "old vines" (Sonoma, California) ..$16
5. David Bruce (Santa Cruz Mountains, California) ..$18
6. Deloach Estate (Napa, California) $19
7. Sky (Napa, California) $23
8. Buehler (Napa, California) $24
9. Gallo-Sonoma Frei Ranch (Sonoma, California) ...$25
10. Storybook Mountain Estate Reserve
    (Napa, California) $29

Good White Zinfandel

1. Talus (California) $6
2. Beringer (California) $7
3. Buehler (Napa, California) $8
4. Deloach (Napa, California) $9

White Zinfandel is the wine of choice for people who otherwise would not drink wine. The noticeable residual sugar (around 1.5 percent), lower alcohol content (10 percent or so), and fresh strawberry fruit flavor give white Zinfandel its broad appeal.

There are several white Zinfandels of quality on the market. The key to good white Zinfandel lies in the color. While many of the palest pink versions are rather bland, the darker versions tend to have more fruit flavors.

Zinfandel is a good choice to have with spicy Pacific Rim cuisine because its sweetness can help put out the fire in people's mouths caused by spicy dishes. The uncomplicated flavors of white Zinfandel, and of most rosés for that matter, are a good match with the intricate seasonings of Far-Eastern cuisine.

Nebbiolo

Main growing regions:	Piedmont (Italy), some California
Aromas and flavors:	Raspberries, plums, and earth
Acidity:	High
Tannin:	Prominent in youth, "dusty" with age
Body:	Medium
Major mixing partners:	None (Some minor, local grapes are blended with Nebbiolo in certain Piedmont wines.)

Named for the dense fogs so prevalent in the vineyards of Piedmont, Italy, the Nebbiolo grape is responsible for several of Italy's—and the world's—finest red wines. The great red wines of Piedmont—Barolo, Barbaresco, Ghemme, Gattinara—are regarded by afficionados as members of the exclusive club of the greatest wines in the world.

In the past the best of these wines, like many Cabernet Sauvignons, were too tannic to drink in their youth and required a decade or so of mellowing. Perhaps more than any other variety, Nebbiolo rewards patience. However, more Nebbiolo-based wines are being vinified to be enjoyable in their youth. If you want an affordable way to get to know Nebbiolo, try an entry-level Barolo or a Nebbiolo d'Alba selected by a wine merchant or reviewer you trust. Unfortunately, entry level for these wines is $10–15. If you see one of these wines from the great year of 1990, it may be a bargain, even if it is a little out of your normal price range.

Despite their powerful flavors, Barolo and other Nebbiolo-based Italian wines need to be served with food because they are quite acidic. Indeed, most Italian wines, red and white, belong at the dinner table, not the coffee table. The California versions have more fruit flavor, which cuts the prominent acidity somewhat. The Italian Nebbiolos are a natural match with rich, earthy dishes such as game and red meat with mushrooms. Even chicken can hold its own with most of these wines.

Look for Piedmont Nebbiolos to be very dry, flavorful but not heavy on the palate, and surprisingly subtle and complex. Look for the California version, which should become

Good Italian Nebbiolo
1. Dessilani Spanna (Piedmont, Italy) $10
2. Filipetti Nebbiolo d'Alba $11
3. Vietti Nebbiolo d'Alba $20
4. Monsecco Le Colline Barbaresco $25
5. Fontanafredda Barolo $30

more prevalent in the years ahead, to have stronger plum and raspberry fruit flavors than those from Italy.

Sangiovese

Main growing regions:	Tuscany (Italy), some California
Aromas and flavors:	Cherries, raisins, earth, and violets
Acidity:	Moderate to high
Tannin:	Moderate
Body:	Light to medium
Major mixing partners:	Cabernet Sauvignon (Italy) and Cannaiolo Nero (Italy)

Sangiovese is an Italian grape that, like the Nebbiolo, hasn't made a significant impact on the wine world when grown outside of Italy. It is the most important grape variety in central Italy, especially in Tuscany. The Brunello and Sangiovetto grapes are close enough relatives of Sangiovese that they are usually considered to be Sangiovese itself.

It might be said that, in terms of style, Sangiovese is to Nebbiolo as Pinot Noir is to Cabernet Sauvignon. Like the great Pinot Noirs of Burgundy, great Sangiovese-based wines from Tuscany—Chianti Classico, Brunello di Montalcino—are somewhat light in body and color yet can improve for many years in the bottle. Also like these great Burgundies, many of these same great Sangiovese wines can be perfectly enjoyable before their fifth birthday.

Like all great varietals, Sangiovese can be a prince or a pauper, and the pauper, a varietal-labeled

I FIND IT HAS AN OPULENT BOUQUET BUT WITH A TOUCH OF IMPUDENCE

Sangiovese from one of Italy's many regions, is frequently a bargain. So far, California winemakers have had a difficult time getting Sangiovese acclimated to the warmth and sunshine of their vineyards. However, a few producers have produced some good Sangioveses.

Sangiovese with a varietal label can be surprisingly inexpensive. Look for the typical cherry fruit, high acid, and low tannin and glycerine. Because of this combination of characteristics, Sangiovese has few equals as a red wine to accompany seafood. When matching food and wine, remember also to match price along with other characteristics. In this sense, inexpensive, varietally labeled Sangiovese is a good pizza and spaghetti wine. These wines are usually better than those inexpensive, silly-looking, straw-covered bottles of cheap Chianti you see at Italian restaurants.

In Chianti wines, the Sangiovese grape has historically been blended with the local Cannaiolo grape as well as two white grapes:

Good Sangiovese

1. Lirico Sangiovese (Veneto, Italy) $6
2. Moris Farms Morellino di Scansano (Tuscany, Italy)$8
3. Conti Contini Sangiovese (Tuscany, Italy) $11
4. Il Cuore Rosso Classico
   (Sangiovese/Zinfandel blend; California) $11
5. Rabbit Ridge Sangiovese (Sonoma, California) ...$13
6. Castello di Gabbiano Chianti Classico
   (Tuscany, Italy) $13
7. Fattoria di Ama Chianti Classico (Tuscany, Italy) .$20
8. Swanson Sangiovese (Napa, California) $20
9. Avignonese Vino Nobile di Montepulciano
   (Tuscany, Italy) $20
10. Antinori Tignanello (Sangiovese/Cabernet Sauvignon
    blend; Tuscany, Italy) $60
11. Biondi-Santi Brunello di Montalcino 1990 ....$100

Trebbiano and Malvasia. Presently, the top producers are omitting the white grapes, in favor of more Sangiovese.

The "super-Tuscan" red wines that first came to the market in the 1980s are a blend of Sangiovese and Cabernet Sauvignon. These

superior wines lie outside of Italy's wine classification system, but they are more intensely flavored than Chianti and are worth a try if you are looking to splurge.

The great Chianti Classico and Brunello di Montalcino wines go well with veal, beef, lamb, and hearty chicken dishes. Sangiovese-based wines also stand up well with tomato sauce. Super Tuscans, with their sturdy framework of Cabernet Sauvignon, are generally best reserved for red meat and game.

Grenache

Main growing regions: Spain, Rhône (France), and California

Aroma and flavor: Raspberry

Acidity: Moderate

Body: Medium to full

Major mixing partners: Syrah (France) and Tempranillo (Spain)

The southern Rhône valley of France is
famous for its sturdy, drinkable and affordable
red wines. Many different grape varieties are
grown here, but Grenache is the predominant
variety and is the primary grape among the
many used to make Côtes-du-Rhône rouge.
This popular wine has ample body, meaty
structure, and a straightforward fruit flavor of
raspberry jam. Côtes-du-Rhône is a genuine
bargain among French red wines, usually
retailing for less than $10 per bottle. The dry

rosés of the neighboring Provence region are also made primarily from the Grenache grape and are considered by many experts to be the finest pink wines in the world.

Under the local name Garnacha, Grenache is extensively planted in Spain and Portugal. It lends fruit to the relatively austere

Good Grenache

1. Jaboulet Côtes-du-Rhône "Parallel 45" (Rhône, France) $10
2. Rabbit Ridge Grenache (Sonoma, California) $11
3. McDowell Valley Vineyards Grenache Rosé (California) $11
4. M. Chapoutier Côtes-du-Rhône "cuvée de Belleruche" (Rhône, France) $12
5. Guigal Tavel Rosé (Rhône, France) $13
6. Guigal Gigondas (Rhône, France) $20
7. Château Rayas Châteauneuf-du-Pape (Rhône, France) $150

Tempranillo grape in the red wines of Rioja (Spain). In California it is vinified in bulk for use in rosés and red jug wines. California Grenache varietal wines, although scarce, can be quite good.

Well-made Grenache-based wines tend to have enough body and character to be enjoyable with or without food. Hearty beef and lamb dishes, especially stews made with Côtes-du-Rhône as an ingredient, seem to bring out the delightful spiciness in Grenache. The most powerful versions of Châteauneuf-du-Pape stand up well to steak au poivre and other powerfully seasoned dishes, whereas tamer bottlings match well with goose, duck, and the like—not summer food, and not summer wine. In hot weather, try pairing a French Tavel or a California rosé with a salad or simple picnic fare.

Gamay

Main growing region: Beaujolais (France)

Aromas and flavors: Strawberries and raspberries

Acidity: Low to moderate

Tannin: Low

Body: Light

Major mixing partners: None

The granite soil of the Beaujolais, the southernmost subregion of Burgundy, brings out the best qualities of the Gamay grape. The red wine of Beaujolais is fresh, light, and fruity, and it is enjoyed all over the world. The lively fruit flavors—strawberry and raspberry—show well in the absence of substantial tannin.

A Gamay-based wine can take a slight chilling and may be offered with just about any food, from poached salmon to barbecued pork ribs. These wines are also enjoyable alone.

The Gamay grape reaches its summit of quality in the "*cru* Beaujolais" wines. These are red wines produced from Gamay grapes grown within the ten townships regarded as superior to the rest of the subregion. It has been observed that these wines, unlike other wines from Beaujolais, can benefit from two or three years of aging.

California does produce, albeit sparingly, two wines whose names imply Gamay—Napa Gamay and Gamay Beaujolais. Napa Gamay is actually the lowly Gros Auxerrois grape from southwest France, and Gamay Beaujolais is an inferior mutation of Pinot Noir. For price and quality, stick to the French version, especially during the Nouveau season when California "Gamay Nouveau" labels are intentionally deceiving and the wines are decidedly inferior to the real thing.

Georges Duboeuf is the king of Beaujolais wines. The quality and pricing of these wines are more than fair. Louis Jadot is another reliable bottler of Beaujolais. This firm bottles all manner of wine from this sub-region— Beaujolais Nouveau, Beaujolais-Villages, and all of the *cru*s.

Tempranillo

Main growing region: Rioja (Spain)

Aromas and flavors: Not very fruity; leather, spice, cherries, and raisins

Acidity: Low to moderate

Tannin: Low to moderate

Body: Medium

Major mixing partner: Grenache/Garnacha (Rioja)

One rarely sees Tempranillo bottled as a varietal, but it is included here because of the importance of Rioja, an affordable treasure from Spain. The inexpensive versions often display the body of Pinot Noir without the flashy fruit. The subtle cherry fruit of Tempranillo is often well masked by smoke flavors and oakiness. Grenache (Garnacha) is the minority blending partner in Rioja, and it adds some fruitiness to the wine. The greatest Rioja cost as much as any great wine and show a depth and length of flavors that justify their price.

As a light- to medium-bodied red with modest acidity, red Rioja matches well with grilled fish, well-seasoned vegetable dishes, and pasta, and also goes well with chicken and red meats.

Good Tempranillo

1. Tempranillo $7
2. Bodegas Montecillo Cumbrero Tinto $9
3. Campo Viejo Crianza a Tinto $15
4. Bodegas Montecillo Reserva $22
5. Marques de Riscal Tinto Gran Reserva $35
6. Vega Sicilia Unico 1970 . . . .$250

The Tempranillo-based Rioja wines are a great value, and they are easy to appreciate. Rioja is a good place for the neophyte to start in his or her exploration of red wine.

Chardonnay

Main growing regions:	Burgundy (France), California, Oregon, Washington State, Australia, South Africa, Chile
Aromas and flavors:	Varies greatly by region; peas, vanilla, tropical fruits, toast, and nuts
Acidity:	Moderate to high
Body:	Light to moderate
Major mixing partner:	Semillon (Australia)

The wine-drinking public is so accustomed to saying, "I'll have a Chardonnay!" that it is worth a reminder that Chardonnay is the name of a white-wine grape variety. In fact,

Chardonnay is the most popular and most versatile white grape in the world.

Chardonnay grapes are used to make the austere, bone-dry wines of France's Chablis subregion; they are truly great seafood wines. Chardonnay is a crucial component of Champagne and the sole grape in the premium Champagne labeled Blanc de Blancs. Chardonnay makes the great white Burgundies from France—the most expensive dry white wines in the world.

It also makes the best white wines in California; they are fruity and sometimes syrupy, high in alcohol, and often framed in oak. Chardonnay can even accommodate a dose of noble rot and yield a gloriously rich and sweet dessert wine. Finally, Chardonnay blends well with other grapes, especially

with Semillon, as commonly blended in
Australia.

Chardonnay displays a propensity for
both glycerine and acid, whose interplay

Good Chardonnay

1. Monterey Vineyard Chardonnay
   (Monterey, California) $7
2. Georges Duboeuf Saint-Véran
   (Macon, Burgundy, France) $10
3. Meridian Chardonnay (Santa Barbara, California) .$10
4. Kendall-Jackson Vintners Reserve Chardonnay
   (California) $14
5. Cambria "Katherine's Vineyard" Chardonnay
   (Santa Barbara, California) $18
6. Robert Mondavi Chardonnay (Napa, California) ..$21
7. Rosemount "Show Reserve" Chardonnay
   (Australia) $24
8. Matanzas Creek Chardonnay (Sonoma, California) $37
9. Hanzell Chardonnay (Sonoma, California) $45
10. Domaine Leflaive Puligny-Montrachet
    (Burgundy, France) $55

results in the most velvety, sensually delightful texture of all white wines. Texture is what one looks for in even simple Chardonnays. Unlike the red-wine kingpin Cabernet Sauvignon, Chardonnays can be of high quality in the $8–10 price range.

The astringent flavor imparted by oak barrels marries well with Chardonnay in different regions. So well, in fact, that it can be difficult to separate in one's mind the flavor of the grape and the flavor of the oak. If you want to taste a pure, unoaked Chardonnay, look for a California Chardonnay that is labeled "Stainless Steel Fermented." This implies no oak.

The Burgundy subregion of Côte de Beaune produces beautifully structured Chardonnay that are brilliant and clean, with acidity, mouth-filling body, and aromas of toast, nuts, butter, and a variety of subtle fruits. When ripened in the California sunshine, the fruit aroma becomes more apparent.

Napa Valley, the first California appellation to excel with Chardonnay tends to produce high-glycerine, well-oaked versions with ample fruit—apple and pear aromas intermingled with oak is a frequent observation. Drive over the Mayacamas mountain range into the Sonoma Valley and you will find a more tropical element in Chardonnay, usually pineapple. The Santa Barbara growing area, far south of Napa/Sonoma, tends to bottle an even riper Chardonnay. The fruit

impression there is even more tropical, and the acidity profile is soft. For yet more fruit flavor, you must go to Australia.

The grape-growing climate in Australia is unique to wine-producing countries. The Hunter Valley in southeastern Australia experiences intense sunshine. This would normally over-ripen wine grapes, but the ripening effect of the sun in this region is greatly tempered by cool breezes. This combination of plentiful sunlight and refreshing air brings grapes to a full ripeness slowly, so as to develop the most intense flavors imaginable in Chardonnay. Suggestions of pineapple, coconut, and bananas spring forth from this deep-golden wine. These wines used to lack the necessary acidity, but innovative winemaking techniques seem to have solved this problem.

Because Chardonnay has such a range of styles, one needs to consider the type of Chardonnay when trying to find the right wine for a particular meal. Chablis is the driest, most acidic interpretation, and belongs with seafood, especially shellfish and delicate white fish like Dover sole. The rounder white Burgundies from the Côte de Beaune are also seafood wines but can accompany meats such as chicken and veal. Seafood doesn't match so well with fruitier Chardonnays such as those from California and Australia.

If you insist on a fruity Chardonnay with your fish, California cuisine comes into play. The flavorful ingredients used in California cuisine—generous additions of fresh herbs and various chili peppers, and wood grilling—can transform a delicate piece of fish into a jam session of loud flavors. A big wine is called for; California Chardonnay is ideal. In fact, big Chardonnays like these can stand up to many dishes not normally paired with white wine—even grilled meats!

Finally, if you want to drink Chardonnay without food, the Australian versions, with their generous fruit and mild acidity, are an excellent choice.

Sauvignon Blanc

Main growing regions: Bordeaux (France), Loire (France), California, Washington State, and South Africa

Aromas and flavors: Cut grass, herbs, and lemon

Acidity: High

Body: Medium

Major mixing partner: Semillon (Bordeaux)

In comparison to Chardonnay, it may take a little more wine knowledge to appreciate a great Sauvignon Blanc. That is because the hallmark of quality Sauvignon Blanc—bright, crisp acidity—is not as sensually pleasing as the seductive texture of good Chardonnay. Yet this high acidity makes for a great pairing with seafood. "Grassy" and "herbaceous" are common descriptions of Sauvignon Blanc's fruit components.

An alternative vinification style of Sauvignon Blanc yields a richer wine. "Fumé Blanc" is the name for a style created in California in the 1960s by Robert Mondavi. Styled after the legendary Pouilly Fumé of the Loire region in France, Fumé Blanc has a richer, fuller style.

Whereas the Sauvignon Blancs are excellent with seafood, the more substantial Fumé Blanc may be paired with a wider variety of dishes, including chicken, veal, and pasta.

There are a few world-class wines made from Sauvignon Blanc that earn this variety its place beside the other white noble grapes,

Good Sauvignon Blanc

1. Kronendaal Sauvignon Blanc (South Africa) $6
2. Canyon Road Sauvignon Blanc (California) $8
3. Matua Valley Sauvignon Blanc (New Zealand) $10
4. Sterling Sauvignon Blanc (Napa, California) $15
5. Michel Redde Sancerre (Loire, France) $18
6. Frog's Leap Sauvignon Blanc (Napa, California) . .$20
7. Duckhorn Sauvignon Blanc (Napa, California) $20
8. Robert Mondavi Fumé Blanc Reserve
   (Napa, California) $24
9. Pouilly Fumé La Doucette (Loire, France) $30
10. Pavillon Blanc du Château Margaux
    (Bordeaux, France) $45

Riesling and Chardonnay. Château Haut-Brion Blanc of Graves is universally regarded as the finest of its type and an equal to the great white Burgundies. Close on its heels is Domaine de  Chevalier, also from Graves. Sauvignon Blanc is blended with a lesser amount of Semillon in most Graves whites. This formula is reversed in the dessert wines from neighboring Sauternes.

In spite of its legitimate claim to nobility, Sauvignon Blanc might well have an inferiority complex. The public hasn't taken to this variety as it has to Chardonnay. Some winemakers have even employed a heavy-handed oaking to make Sauvignon Blanc seem more like Chardonnay. Fortunately, low demand has kept the prices down somewhat. Try serving

a good Sauvignon Blanc with an uncomplicated seafood dish without telling your guests
what they are drinking. You will look very
wine smart.

Riesling

Main growing regions: Germany, Alsace (France), and California

Aromas and flavors: Apricots, citrus, peaches, and flowers

Acidity: Moderate to high

Body: Light; medium to heavy for dessert wines

Major mixing partners: None (Riesling is often blended with lesser varieties in nonvarietal German QbA wines.)

Just as Pinot Noir rivals Cabernet Sauvignon
for preeminence among noble red varieties,
the Riesling grape has a following who regard
it as superior to Chardonnay. Like Pinot Noir,

Riesling has not traveled as well as its rival. Both Pinot Noir and Riesling turn shy in the warmth of California and require a cooler climate in order to perform well. Whereas the demand for quality Pinot Noir has motivated American winemakers to seek out promising vineyards for it, Riesling has never been in high demand in the United States. Riesling's alleged sweetness has also kept it out of the fast lane in today's wine market. Riesling grapes can make sweet wine. Their prominent acidity provides the perfect balance for late-harvest sweetness, and they can produce the sweetest dessert wines in the world. However, some excellent Rieslings, notably those from Alsace, can be nearly bone dry. The aroma of well-made Riesling is flowery as well as fruity. Riesling *smells* sweeter than Chardonnay.

Riesling has long been the basis for the finest wines of Germany. The steep slopes

Good Riesling

1. Ste. Chapelle Dry Riesling (Idaho) $6
2. Bernkastler Kurfurstlay QbA
   (Mosel-Saar-Ruwer, Germany) $7
3. Bornheimer Adelberg Kabinett (Reinhessen,
   Germany) $8
4. Geyser Peak Soft Johannisberg Riesling
   (Sonoma, California) $8
5. Hermann J. Wiemer Dry Riesling (New York) $9
6. Trimbach Riesling (Alsace, France) $16
7. Trefethen White Riesling (Napa, California) $18
8. Charles Schleret Riesling "Herrenweg"
   (Alsace, France) $18
9. J. J. Prum Wehlener Sonnenhur Spätlese
   (Mosel-Saar-Ruwer) $30
10. Domaine Weinbach Riesling Alsace Cuvee
    Ste. Catherine $50

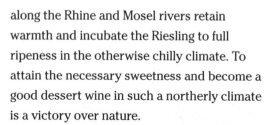

along the Rhine and Mosel rivers retain warmth and incubate the Riesling to full ripeness in the otherwise chilly climate. To attain the necessary sweetness and become a good dessert wine in such a northerly climate is a victory over nature.

Some of the best values in the wine world today are the German Rieslings designated QbA and labeled "Riesling." The superior QmP white wines from Germany are by definition made from Riesling unless labeled otherwise.

There have been some notable successes with Riesling in North America, many outside of California. Oregon, Washington State, Idaho, New York, and Canada all produce quality Rieslings.

Be wary of imitations! Several lowly grape varieties, including Gray Riesling and Welschriesling, are deceptively named and have nothing to do with the real thing. Look for wines labeled "Riesling," "White Riesling," or "Johannisberg Riesling." Don't be afraid of an older bottle. Rieslings have demonstrated a capacity to improve with age, much more so than Chardonnays. This is especially true of the Alsace and German Rieslings.

Chenin Blanc

Main growing regions:	Loire (France), South Africa, New Zealand, and California
Aromas and flavors:	Somewhat muted; bread, pine, and orange
Acidity:	Very high
Body:	Light to medium
Major mixing partner:	Chardonnay

Chenin Blanc is widely grown around the world and has several distinct personalities. In the Loire Valley of northwestern France, where it has been cultivated for over a thousand years, Chenin Blanc is responsible for the acidic white wines of Anjou and Touraine. The best known of these is Vouvray, which itself can take several forms.

Vouvray, whose name comes from the village in Touraine where it is produced, is probably the most weather-sensitive table wine in the world. Whereas winemakers elsewhere usually attempt to produce a somewhat consistent style from vintage to vintage, Vouvray is made in very different styles depending on the weather. A pleasant, sunny summer brings the Chenin Blanc grapes in Vouvray to full ripeness. In such years demi-sec (half-dry) wine is usually produced. These wines have a pleasant level of residual sugar, but they are dry enough to enjoy with dinner. Chenin Blanc's inherent bracing acidity provides ample balance to the sweetness in demi-sec wines. These wines match well with a wide variety of light dishes.

A cold and rainy summer is unwelcome in any vineyard. Rather than gnash their teeth, though, the winemakers of Vouvray respond by making Vouvray sec. This dry version of Chenin Blanc is very acidic. Such wine is nearly impossible to drink without food and is difficult to match with anything other than shellfish.

Vouvray sec does have a following, however, among connoisseurs who prize naked acidity. On the other end of the sweetness spectrum is Quarts de Chaume, a melony, honeyed dessert wine made from *Botrytis*-affected Chenin Blanc from Anjou in the Loire Valley. These sweet wines are said to live indefinitely in the bottle, as do the sweeter versions of the Vouvray demi-sec.

High acidity is the backbone of well-made sparkling wine, and the naturally acidic Chenin Blanc grape is used to make high-quality sparkling wine in the Loire region. Semi-sparkling wine labeled "Vouvray Mousseux" is common, and the great Champagne firm of Taittinger produces its Bouvet Brut from Chenin Blanc in the Loire.

Good Chenin Blanc

1. Landskroon Steen (South Africa) $8
2. Matua Valley Chenin Blanc/Chardonnay
   (New Zealand) $9
3. Dry Creek Chenin Blanc (Sonoma, California) $10
4. B&G Vouvray (Loire, France) $10
5. Mark Bredif Vouvray (Loire, France) $14
6. Domaine Baumard Quarts de Chaume
   (Loire, France) $50

These sparkling wines, though not as complex as true Champagne, are often as well made and offer excellent value.

Chenin Blanc has traveled abroad with success. It was brought to South Africa in the 1600s by Dutch settlers and is widely grown there under the name of Steen. In California, Chenin Blanc is extensively cultivated for use in brandy-making and as part of the mix in jug wines.

There have also been many pleasant and enjoyable California Chenin Blancs sold as varietal wines, but their popularity is fading. The best of these display the same honey and melon aromas as Quarts de Chaume with moderate acidity—perfect summer wines. Chenin Blanc is sometimes blended with Chardonnay in New Zealand and in Loire.

In general, Chenin Blanc–based wines match well with summer foods. Because of their high acidity, restrained fruit, and balance, well-made versions can be a welcome respite from your usual white wine. These wines have a natural affinity with sweet shellfish like sea scallops, but are also enjoyable with anything light, such as pasta, fish, and chicken.

Pinot Blanc

Main growing regions: Burgundy (France), Alsace (France), Italy, and California

Aromas and flavors: Somewhat subdued almonds and apples

Acidity: Moderate to high

Body: Medium to full

Major mixing partner: Chardonnay (Burgundy)

Also known as Pinot Bianco in Italy, Pinot Blanc is known for its simple, full-bodied, clean structure and forward acidity. It is used (in combination with other grapes) for some premium sparkling wines in California. Not widely produced in California, Pinot Blanc can be a good value among Alsace wines. Because it usually makes a relatively uncomplicated wine, Pinot Blanc is enjoyable with a wide variety of dishes and does not require particularly careful matching.

Good Pinot Blanc

1. White Burgundy (Monterey, California) $9
2. Hugel "cuvée les Amours" Pinot Blanc
   (Alsace, France) $12
3. Eno Friulia Pinot Bianco (Friuli, Italy) $12
4. Chalone Pinot Blanc (Monterey, California) $27

Originally cultivated in ancient Burgundy, Pinot Blanc has long been cultivated side by side with Chardonnay. Indeed, some mutations of Pinot Blanc are capable of producing a Chardonnay-like wine. But for the most part, Pinot Blanc makes a rather nondescript wine with weak aroma—good with food and boring without. Although we encourage occasional daring and uninformed purchases in the wine store, for Pinot Blanc we suggest you start with our recommended bottles.

Semillon

Main growing regions: Bordeaux (France), Australia, and California

Aromas and flavors: Figs, honey, and lemon

Acidity: Low to medium

Body: Full

Major mixing partners: Chardonnay (Australia) and Sauvignon Blanc (Bordeaux)

The Semillon grape rarely stands alone as a varietal. It is often blended in the Graves subregion of Bordeaux, France, with Sauvignon Blanc. Its silky richness complements the acidity of the Sauvignon Blanc. In Australia Semillon is used in Semillon/Chardonnay blends. These wines are pleasant and inexpensive.

Good Semillon

1. Penfolds Semillon/Chardonnay Koonunga Hill (Australia) $8
2. Indian Hill Semillon (Sierra Foothills, California) ..$10
3. Château Haut-Gravier (Graves, France) $11
4. Peter Lehmann Sauternes-Semillon (Australia) ....$13/half bottle
5. Château Raymond-Lafon (Sauternes, France) ....$25/half bottle

Semillon is the main variety in Sauternes, the dessert wine–producing sub-region of Bordeaux. These wines also have Sauvignon Blanc mixed in to give them a  little acidity. Good and affordable dessert Semillon, in its pure form, is produced in Australia.

Its signature characteristics are low acidity and thick body, and its aromas and flavors of figs, honey, and lemon are restrained. This set of qualities does not add up to an exceptional table wine, but good, inexpensive varietal Semillon is available. However, Semillon's propensity for richness and its susceptibility to "noble rot" make it a useful grape variety, albeit one with limited applications.

Viognier

Main growing regions: Rhône (France) and California

Aromas and flavors: Apricots, wood, peaches, and flowers

Acidity: Low to medium

Body: Medium to full

Major mixing partners: None

The unheralded Viognier grape has been producing some fine alternatives to Chardonnay in France's upper Rhône. Viognier's popularity is fairly recent as a varietal from California. Its apricot/peach flavors are a refreshing alternative to the repetitive pear/vanilla flavors of California Chardonnay. In fact, Viognier's biggest asset may be its vastly different flavor structure compared to Chardonnay, making it a good choice for those seeking an alternative to Chardonnay.

The northern Rhône valley of Condrieu is the home turf for Viognier. The Viognier grape approaches world-class status here: A bottle of Château Grillet fetches $100 or more, and is said to age well *forever* in the bottle. Less expensive but certainly note-

---

Good Viognier Blanc

1. Georges Duboeuf Viognier (France) $9
2. B&G Viognier (France) $10
3. Rabbit Ridge Viognier (Sonoma, California) $16
4. Arrowood Viognier (Sonoma, California) $33
5. Guigal Condrieu (Rhône, France) $33
6. Château Grillet (Condrieu, Rhône, France) $100

worthy versions of Viognier also come from the Condrieu vineyards.

At its best, Viognier has aromas and flavors of peach, apricot, and flowers, though it is not as overtly flowery as Riesling. With the aromas and flavors of these particular fruit, Viognier is a natural match with pork, which has an affinity for both. However, if you substitute Viognier for Chardonnay in any food-wine pairing, you won't be disappointed.

California Viognier is not cheap. For bargains, look for varietal Viognier from big French producers. Inexpensive vin de pays varietal Viognier has caught on in the French countryside, at least for export. These are often good values in terms of quality when compared with similarly priced Chardonnay.

Pinot Grigio/Pinot Gris

Main growing regions: Italy, Alsace (France), Oregon, and California

Aromas and flavors: Somewhat muted; minerals, pine, and orange rind

Acidity: Medium (generally higher in Europe)

Body: Medium (generally heavier in the United States)

Major mixing partners: None

A close relative of Pinot Blanc, Pinot Grigio has recently become a very popular varietal wine from Italy. In Friuli and Aldo Adige, two northern regions of Italy, Pinot Grigio can produce a well-structured and acidic match for seafood, with somewhat muddled aromas. In warmer climates, however, the acidity level can be undesirably low. Pinot Grigio is a relatively recent visitor to California, where it has yet to succeed in making wines comparable to those in northern Italy.

Alsatian soil brings out the best in several white varieties, and Pinot Grigio, known there as Tokay Pinot Gris, is one of them. This pink-skinned variety is not very strong-willed and is a perfect vehicle for the Alsace *terroir*— rich, minerally soil flavors mingle with the substantial acidity.

Good Pinot Grigio/Pinot Gris

1. Lirica Pinot Grigio (Veneto, Italy) $6
2. Castello d'Albola Pinot Grigio (Tuscany, Italy) $9
3. Eno Friulia Pinot Grigio (Friuli, Italy) $13
4. Gustave Lorenz Pinot Gris Reserve
   (Alsace, France) $15
5. Eyrie Vineyard Pinot Gris (Oregon) $17
6. Puiatti Pinot Grigio (Friuli, Italy) $22

The Oregonians call their version Pinot Gris. The cool Williamette Valley appears to be a Pinot Gris–friendly growing region. These wines have stronger than usual Pinot Gris flavor, rich body, and the signature pine and orange aromas of Pinot

Grigio. These wines tend to be more expensive than the Italian versions.

Because it doesn't have prominent fruit flavors, Pinot Grigio is relatively easy to match with food. The drier, more acidic versions are excellent with shellfish and other seafoods, whereas the fuller-bodied versions can accompany chicken and pasta dishes well.

Gewürztraminer

Main growing regions:	Germany, Alsace (France), and California
Aromas and flavors:	Strong lychee-nut fruit and grapefruit rind
Acidity:	Low to medium
Body:	Full
Major mixing partners:	None

A mouthful, literally, Gewürztraminer (gah-VERTS-truh-MEEN-er) can be as difficult to enjoy as it is to pronounce. Rich, pungent, spicy flavors with fruit notes of lychee and grapefruit rind make for a difficult food-wine pairing. As such, Gewürztraminer is often suggested with spicy Asian food—an awkward blind date at best. Regional tradition in Alsace matches Gewürztraminer with sausage and ham. Because of its low acidity and bold flavors, Gewürztraminer can be enjoyable all by itself, without food. Alternatively, a simple, creamy cheese provides a good background for the complex, full personality of this grape.

Gewürztraminer is a pink-skinned clone of the much older Traminer vine that probably originated in northern Italy. The "Gewürz-" is

---

Good Gewürztraminer

1. Geyser Peak Gewürztraminer (Sonoma, California) $8
2. Durkheimer Feuerberg Gewürztraminer QbA
   (Rheinfalz, Germany) $11
3. Chateau St. Jean Gewürztraminer
   (Sonoma, California) $12
4. Charles Schleret Gewürztraminer "Herrenweg"
   (Alsace, France) $18
5. Domaine Zind-Humbrecht Gewürztraminer
   Turckheim (Alsace, France) $33

German for "spicy" or "pungent" and reflects the powerful aromas of Gewürztraminer wines. It is the least subtle of all the well-known *vinifera* grapes.

Although it grows best in Alsace (France), it plays second fiddle there to the Riesling grape. Its share of vineyard space in Germany has been on the decline, again being out-muscled by the Riesling grape. California and Pacific Northwest versions of this quirky variety tend to lack the complexity of their European counterparts, but can be both enjoyable and affordable.

Minor Grapes

The *Vitis vinifera* family of grapes, which is responsible for wine as we know it, is indeed a very large family. There are thousands of such grape varieties, yet most are unknown to wine drinkers and wine-store shelves. Vines grow all over the world, but relatively few varieties are used for the commercial production of wine. The well-known wine grapes are famous because they produce good or balanced wine, and to grow them requires little-to-reasonable effort.

There are some grapes that are used as blending grapes for the family big wigs. This is done to make a wine taste less tannic or acidic, to make it more complex, to save money, or any combination of these reasons. The minor wine grapes used in commercial wine production are often red grapes that are blended with other red grapes. Cabernet Franc, although rarely found alone, is considered by many to be Cabernet Sauvignon's best friend.

Malbec is a more typical example of a minor grape. It is used in wine production throughout the world. Malbec makes simple, sturdy wine. The skins and seeds are thoroughly removed from the juice of this and

Some Minor Varieties Worth Looking For:

Red

Barbera (Piedmont, Italy)

Malbec (Argentina; originally from Bordeaux, France)

Lemberger (Washington State; originally from Germany)

Carmenere (Chile; originally from Bordeaux, France)

Periquita (Portugal)

White

Grüner Veltliner (Austria)

Aligoté (Burgundy, France)

Sylvaner (Germany)

Furmint (Hungary)

Chasselas (Switzerland)

most of the other minor commercial grapes. This is because the flavors of the acids and tannins are not as desirable in the minor grapes as those of the major grapes like Cabernet Sauvigon. Remember, the skins of red-wine grapes give a wine some of its signature characteristics. If people liked the signature characteristics of Malbec, Cinsault, Cannaiolo, Kerner, and the many other grapes most people have never heard of, then we'd be drinking wines featuring those grapes.

Don't dismiss these grapes as meaningless. Some of the famous wines of Italy, France, and Spain have some minor grapes blended  in for the sole purpose of making the wine better. Different countries have different laws concerning the legal percentages of these grapes in the wine. A grape variety that accounts for 5–25 percent of a wine, depending on the country, doesn't need to be credited. Of course, most European wines don't even credit the star grape on the wine label.

There are relatively minor grapes from which wines are made, but they are rarely sold outside the region in which they are produced. In Germany, the easy-to-grow and early-ripening Müller-Thurgau grape is made into a simple white wine enjoyed mostly in Germany. In Argentina, Criolla is used to make a simple

white wine for Argentineans to enjoy. The red Periquita grape is popular in Portugal.

Italy is by far the biggest producer of decent Barbera, which makes a very drinkable, food-friendly red wine. It's a good pizza wine, and it is currently enjoying some success outside of the homeland. Italy also has many lesser known grape varieties that are used to produce wine for the locals.

The Muscadet grape of Loire, France, is a grape that is used to make wines that go well with shellfish. It is hardly ever grown elsewhere.

Spain's white Arien grape, the most widely planted wine grape in the world, is unfamiliar as a variety to most wine buffs.

These minor grape varieties have a few things in common. For the most part, they

have not found a worldwide following because
they lack distinctive, high-quality characteristics. They do grow easily in their home
regions, where they have long been enjoyed as
inexpensive everyday wines. As such, they
tend well with the local cuisine, and that is
probably the best way to enjoy them. If they
are well made, they can be excellent values.
Several of these varieties have been successfully transplanted to the New World and are
becoming popular as varietal wines.

CHAPTER 4

Special Occasion Wines

Sparkling Wine (Champagne)

The bubbles in Champagne and sparkling wines set them apart from all other wines, lending a sense of frivolity and joyousness not otherwise associated with wine-drinking. Champagne has long been virtually a requirement for celebrations such as New Year's Eve, sports victories, and weddings. People who normally do not drink wine nonetheless enjoy Champagne at such occasions. Presently, however, the wine boom has not extended to Champagne and sparkling wines; as the wine-drinking public becomes more interested and knowledgeable in the still wines of the world, consumption of bubbly has slackened in favor of demand for Chardonnay and Merlot. It remains for those consumers following this trend to discover that Champagne and sparkling wines are not just for celebrations—they can be as well made, affordable, and appropriate with good food as any other wine.

Sparkling wine starts out as white (or pink) wine. It is then put in a bottle or barrel with yeast and sugar for a second fermentation, which produces a little more alcohol (1 percent of volume) and a lot of carbon dioxide (bubbles). The alcohol kills the yeast, which is eventually removed with great care so as not to lose the carbonation.

The result is white wine or rosé enhanced by natural carbonation and the complex flavors developed during the second fermentation. If the second fermentation occurred in the same bottle in which it is sold, then it was made via the Champagne method, or *méthode champenoise* as it is known in France where it was supposedly invented by the blind monk named Dom Pérignon. This is the best, but most labor-intensive, way of making sparkling wine.

The best sparkling wines in the world, according to the French and many other people, come from Champagne, a wine-producing region in northern France. Only sparkling wines produced in this region via

Champagne & Sparkling Wines Buying Guide

Good Inexpensive Stuff

Feist-Belmont Blanc de Blancs (France) $8

Paul Cheneau Blanc de Blancs (Spain) $9

Domaine St. Michelle (Washington State) $10

Culbertson (California) $10

Bouvet Brut (Loire, France) $11

Rotari Brut Riserva (Italy) $13

Better Less Inexpensive Stuff

Gloria Ferrar Brut (Sonoma, California) $18

Domaine Chandon Brut Cuvee (Napa, California) $19

Scharffenberger Pacific Echo (Mendocino, CA) $22

Best of California

Scharffenberger Blanc de Blancs (Mendocino, CA) . . .$23

Iron Horse Brut (Sonoma, California) $27

Jordan "J" Sparkling Wine (Alexander Valley, CA) $27

Domaine Chandon "Etoile" (Napa, California) $29

Roederer Estate "Brut L'Hermitage"

     (Anderson Valley, California) $40

Schramsberg J. Schram Brut (Napa, California) $54

Recommended French Champagnes

(all from Champagne, France, of course)

Pol Roger Brut $33

Laurent-Perrier Brut $37

Moët et Chandon "White Star" (extra dry) $41

Moët et Chandon Brut Imperial $45

G. H. Mumm "Rene Lalou," 1985 . . . .$65

Champagne for Rock Stars

Perrier-Jouët Flower Bottle, 1989 . . . .$90
Louis Roederer "Cristal," 1989 . . . .$145
Dom Pérignon, 1992 . . . .$150

Champagne for True Connoisseurs

Laurent Perrier Grande Siecle $115
Krug Grand Cuvée $120
Bollinger R. D. Extra Brut $125
Taittinger Comtes de Champagne Blanc de Blancs . .$145
Pol Roger "Cuvée Sir Winston Churchill" $150
Krug (vintage) $195
Salon Le Mesnil $200

Good Pink Stuff, California

Mirabelle Brut Rosé (North Coast) $14
Gloria Ferrar Blanc de Noirs (Sonoma) $15
Mumm Cuvée Napa Blanc de Noirs (Napa) $16
Schramsberg Brut Rosé Cuvée de Pinot (Napa) $29
Iron Horse Rosé Brut (Sonoma) $30

Really Good Pink Stuff, Champagne

Jean Vesselle Brut Rosé $30
Moët et Chandon Vintage Brut Imperial Rosé $60
Billecart-Salmon Rosé $65
Taittinger Comtes de Champagne Brut Rosé $145
Louis Roederer "Cristal" Rosé $220

Sweet Sparkling Wine

Saracco Moscato d'Asti (Piedmont, Italy) $15
Schramsberg Cremant Demi-Sec (Napa, California) . . .$30
Vueve Clicquot Demi-Sec (Champagne, France) $43

the Champagne method are denoted as Champagne. Therefore, the only true Champagne comes from Champagne, France.

Much to the fury of the French, some cheap sparkling wines made in the United States, Canada, and Australia can legally call themselves champagne (with a small "c") in those countries. The French have long jealously guarded this place-name. The treaty of Versailles specifically forbade the Germans from appropriating the name, and the EEC nations honor the French label law.

Sparkling wine should be served well-chilled, so that the carbonation will last longer and feel smoother. However, those who are drinking very expensive Champagne will want to serve it at a slightly warmer temperature so that

they may, at least theoretically, taste why they paid so much for a bottle of sparkling wine.

For around $10–15, pretty good California or Spanish sparkling wine can be had. (Spanish sparkling wine is known as cava.) We consider California sparkling wine to be a very good wine value; it is fruitier and less dry than French versions. If you don't like your sparkling wine to be very dry, you may not even like the real stuff from Champagne.

The driest of Champagnes and sparkling wines often contain a high proportion of Chardonnay and are appropriate with any light seafood dish. Pale bubbly (that is not rosé bubbly) is rarely *incorrect* with any dish. Historically this has been an easy way out of the food-wine matching game for many a host.

Sweet Sparkling Wine

People who don't enjoy dry table wines often do enjoy two types of wine—sweet and sparkling. Sweet sparkling wine offers a way to double their wine-drinking pleasure. The sweetness usually comes from a high amount of added sugar—almost all sparkling wines have at least some sugar added after the dead yeast is removed. Sweet sparkling wine, usually labeled demi-sec, is usually drunk without food, although it matches well with simple creamy cheeses and many desserts.

Pink Champagne/Brut Rosé

The better sparkling wines, including Champagne, are usually made from both green-skinned grapes (Chardonnay) and black-skinned grapes (Pinot Noit and Pinot Meunier). If pigment from the black-skinned grapes is permitted to lend color to the wine, the result is pink-colored sparkling wine, also called brut rosé. There is a broad price spectrum of pink-hued bubbly, ranging from the $4 pink "champagne" (with a plastic cork) from bulk producers in California to exquisite and rare French versions that cost over $200. The growing climate in California brings Pinot Noir to full ripeness and is especially well-suited to the production of affordable and well-made brut rosé. The fuller-bodied of these are sturdy enough to enjoy with traditional red wine dishes such as beef and game birds.

Dessert Wine

Dessert wine is very sweet white wine that usually has a rich golden color. It can be made several ways. In most cases the residual sugar in these sweet wines is the result of the "noble rot," the *Botrytis cinerea* fungus on grapes left on the vine to become overly ripe. This "affliction" draws water from the grapes and adds complex flavors. The resulting crop of grapes has a high concentration of sugar, not all of which converts to alcohol during fermentation. Other types of dessert wines are made from over-ripe grapes that are simply very high in sugar content.

Because the grape juice used to make dessert wines has so much sugar, the fermentation process can potentially produce a high level of alcohol. The high sugar content also helps preserve the wine, so it can improve in the bottle for many years. Unlike most dry white wines, these wines can last for several days after being opened. They are best served at around 50°F (10°C).

If you are interested in trying a dessert wine, you probably should start with a half bottle. Two people together are very unlikely to drink a half bottle in a sitting. In fact, if you are just experimenting, you can probably stretch a half bottle to four people.

These wines are better served alone as dessert, rather than as an accompaniment to dessert. They are often too sweet to match with dessert food. Ironically, they are often served as an appetizer!

In the United States, Sherry and Port may be labeled "dessert wine" even if they are somewhat dry. They are not dessert wines in the same sense. This is one of the many annoying cases of misleading information on wine bottles. Make sure you are getting a real dessert wine. If you have a sweet tooth, you may really find them to be wonderful.

Fortified Wine

There are four primary types of fortified wines: Port, Sherry, Madeira, and Marsala. The popular drinking wines are Port and Sherry. The Madeira and Marsala are better known for being cooking wines, but there are good bottles of each for drinking. "Fortified" refers to the addition of alcohol in the production process. The wine's alcohol content is boosted from 10–14 percent up to 18–20 percent by adding grape brandy that is usually made from the same grape as the original wine.

When brandy is added after fermentation, the fortified wine is dry (has no residual sugar). If added before fermentation is complete, the fortified wine is sweet because the extra alcohol stops the yeast from converting the sugars. Fortified wine runs the gamut from bone-dry Fino Sherry to rich, sweet Port and Madeira. All four of these fortified wines have lengthy stories, as do most things in the wine world.

Port

Port, or Porto, comes from Portugal. The name, however, comes not from the country but from the city of Oporto at the

mouth of the Douro River. As the only red fortified wine it has natural appeal among red
wine lovers who prize Port's capacity to
improve with age in the bottle for many
decades.

Port is sold in several different styles—
Vintage, Tawny, and Ruby are the principal
versions. Vintage Port, the most expensive of
these, is also the easiest to produce—as long
as nature cooperates; Tawny Port, so named
for its brownish cast, is the result of long
barrel-aging; and Ruby Port, named for its
bright unoxidized color, is an inexpensive style that is perfect for neophytes and fine cooking.

Port is made from several different red varieties that grow to
extreme ripeness in Portugal's hot Duro
valley. The fruity Souzão grape, the

dark-colored "Tintas"—Tinta Cao and Tinta Francisca—and the Cabernet franc-like Touriga are blended along with other varieties in various proportions. A white Port is produced, although it is not nearly as prized as the red versions. All (red) Port, then, starts out as "musts" from these varieties, which are allowed to ferment halfway to dryness before the addition of brandy. Since half of the natural sugar remains unfermented, the resulting fortified wine is sweet. It then begins its life in "Port pipes" (138-gallon storage casks).

Vintage Port

After two years in storage a vintage may be "declared" by agreement of a majority of the Port producers. This means that the Port from that particular vintage is deemed to be of sufficient quality to justify offering it as top-of-the-line Vintage Port. Vintage Port is then bottled and is best aged for at least a decade. Because Vintage Port ages in the bottle, often for several decades, it deposits a substantial amount of sediment in the bottle.

Vintage Port has always been quite popular among the British, and a "match made in heaven" is Vintage Port and a wedge of Stilton, the deluxe cheese of England. The pungent saltiness of the cheese complements beautifully the sweet richness of Vintage Port.

Tawny Port

Unlike Vintage Port, which is transferred to bottles in its youth, Tawny Port may remain in the cask for 10, 20, or even 30 years. "Tawny" refers to the pale brown hue of these

Good Dessert Wines

1. Andrew Quady Essencia (California) $11
2. Peter Lehmann Botrytis Semillon Sauternes
   (Australia) $13
3. Ceretto Moscato d'Asti "Santa Stefano"
   (Piedmont, Italy) $13
4. Schramsberg Cremant Demi-Sec (Napa, California)$15
5. Lolonis "Eugenia" Late Harvest Chardonnay
   (Mendocino) $22
6. Château Raymond Lafon Sauternes
   (Bordeaux, France) $25
7. Domaine Coyeaux Muscat
   Beaumes-de-Venise (Rhône, France) $25
8. Veuve Clicquot Demi-Sec Champagne
   (Champagne, France) $43
9. Disznoko Tokaji Aszu 6 Puttonyos
   (Hungary) (500-ml bottle) $45
10. Château des Charmes Riesling Ice Wine
    Bosc Estate (Ontario, Canada) $50
11. Schneider, Niersteiner Hipping
    Trockenbeerenauslese (Rheinhessen, Germany) $175
12. Château d'Yquem Sauternes (Bordeaux, France) $250

fortified wines after so long in the cask, where oxidation occurs more readily than in the bottle. With the high alcohol guarding against the formation of vinegar, the oxidation in this case improves the flavor over time. The fruit flavors of youth evolve into mellower, more subtle flavors, and the Port becomes seemingly less sweet.

Tawny Port requires far more blending skill than does vintage Port. Unless labeled "Port of the Vintage" (another form of Tawny Port), most Tawnys are blends of ports from several different years chosen for their complementary characteristics.

Ruby Port

Ruby Port, named for its bright crimson color, is a blend of young, lesser lots of Port.

Again the blender's art is of importance—lesser lots (casks) of Port may be skillfully blended to produce an inexpensive and delicious Ruby Port.

The forthright flavors of Ruby Port make it a perfect choice for recipes that call for Port—the flavors of Ruby Port will endure the cooking process far better than will the other types. Also, Ruby Port is a perfect introduction to Port as you begin to explore fortified wines.

Sherry

Like the other types of fortified wine, Sherry owes its popularity to the British. In fact, the name "Sherry" is an Anglicization of "Jerez," the port city on the coast of Spain from which Sherry is shipped.

Sherry is made by fortifying dry white wine made from the Palomino grape grown in southern Spain. Among wine lovers, Sherry is not as well respected as Port, perhaps because Sherry is generally less "wine-like" and complex than Port. As a result, quality Sherry is often overlooked and underpriced. And yet, quality Sherry can be an ideal substitute for a variety of hard liquor drinks:

- Serve a well-chilled fino Sherry in place of a martini;
- Offer a dark, dry Oloroso Sherry (at room temperature) after dinner instead of Cognac;
- Replace sweet liqueur with a sweet cream Sherry.

Whereas Port, particularly vintage Port, is perceived as closely akin to fine wine by consumers, quality Sherry is regarded as a manufactured product by many people, more like liquor than wine. Indeed, the aging, fortification, and blending processes for Sherry are far more involved than those for Vintage Port.

All Sherry begins its life in the warm, dry vineyards of southern Spain. Here the Palomino grape, a variety of little use aside from Sherry production, is made into dry, still wine. This wine, called *mosto,* is initially fortified with brandy to an alcohol level of 15 percent and permitted to age in the presence of air. While contact with air would destroy most wines at this stage, the partially forti-fied *mosto* thrives on it. In most (but not all) of these huge barrels, a cushion of spongy yeast, called *flor,* develops on the surface of the wine.

In barrels with ample *flor* development, the wine beneath the layer of yeast is protected from oxidation and remains pale in color. The *flor* yeast also imparts flavor to the wine and further concentrates the alcoholic content. Sherry from these barrels is generally called "fino" and may become one of the three paler types of Sherry—Fino itself, Mauzauilla, or Amontillado.

The barrels that develop little or no *flor* yeast yield "oloroso" Sherry, which is finished as one of the darker styles—dry Oloroso itself, sweet Amoroso, or very sweet cream Sherry. An especially rare type of Sherry is Palo Cortado, an Oloroso that develops *flor* yeast late in its life and can combine the finest qualities of both Finos and Olorosos.

Because the alcohol in Fino Sherries is concentrated by the *flor* yeast, these types of Sherry are given additional fortification only as required by importers worldwide. In Spain, Fino Sherry is often not additionally fortified and can be found at 16 percent alcohol. As such, this type of Sherry will not survive indefinitely in an opened bottle.

The darker Oloroso Sherries usually receive a second fortification that raises the alcoholic strength to 18–20 percent. Because of this, Olorosos can live for a long time in the bottle after it is opened.

The blending process used in Sherry production, called the "solera" process, is unique. Barrels of young Sherry are connected to older barrels in such a manner that Sherries from different years are blended; this is why there are no vintage sherries. You may, however, find an expensive Sherry with a year on the label. This is usually the vintage year of the oldest Sherry in the solera blend and may be over 100 hundred years old.

The Fino Family

Manzanilla—This is a pale, dry, fino Sherry that comes from the coastal town of Sanlúcar de Barrameda. Because it matures in casks stored near the sea, it acquires a tangy salty flavor from the coastal air. Serve it with tapas.

Fino—Fino is both the general name of the unfinished *flor* Sherries and the name of one of the finished products within that group. This Sherry is pale, dry, and best served chilled as an apéritif in the hot summer.

Amontillado—Made famous by an Edgar Alan Poe short story ("The Cask of Amontillado"), this style of Sherry is most notable for its nut-like flavor and aroma. These characteristics, along with a light brown color, can develop when a fino-type Sherry ages. Like the other fino types, Amontillado is a before-dinner drink, though better served at room temperature. While the paler fino types are most enjoyable in the hot summer, Amontillado is something of an autumn apéritif with its darker, richer flavors.

The Oloroso Family

Oloroso—There is a popular perception that

darker Sherries are, by definition, sweeter—
not so. Oloroso Sherry itself is, in its natural
state, quite dry. (Like Fino
Sherry, Oloroso Sherry is
both the name of a cate-
gory of sherries—those
unaffected by *flor*—and the
name of one of the finished
products in this category.

Good Oloroso is dry, richly flavored, and full-
bodied, and is medium-brown in color.

Amoroso—Dry Oloroso Sherry is sometimes sweetened by the addition of sweet,
concentrated wine made for this purpose
from Moscatel or Pedro Ximenez grapes.
The result is Amoroso Sherry, a sweet after-
dinner drink. Similarly, Amoroso may be

darkened by the addition of specially prepared "coloring wine." Brown sherry is an
especially dark version of Amoroso sherry.

Cream—The sweetest of Sherries, if not
the darkest, is Cream Sherry, first developed in Bristol, England. The widespread
success of Harvey's Bristol Cream notwith-
standing, Cream Sherry (even Harvey's!)
can be an enjoyable after-dinner drink.

Madeira and Marsala

Whereas Port and Sherry are generally
enjoyed as beverages, Madeira and
Marsala are more commonly used for
cooking. If you find that you enjoy Sherry
and Port, you might want to experiment
with these.

Madeira

Madeira is a small Portuguese-governed island in the Atlantic Ocean off the north-west coast of Africa that produces fortified wines named after the island. The most common of these wines are used for cooking, but the better ones are consumed as cocktails. The early American colonists used to drink Madeira, so the island has a long history of producing and exporting its goods. Madeira is heated during the production process. It was discovered that heat improved the taste of the wine in the 1600s when Madeira was shipped across the Atlantic in hot cargo ships.

Light brown in color, Maderia can be sweet or dry. The four primary types of Madeira are Sercial, Verdelho, Bual, and Malmsey. If you don't see one of these four

names on the bottle, you are getting a lesser
Madeira. If you are going to venture into the
world of Madeira wines, compare a pale
Sercial to a dark Malmsey and figure out
what style you like. The best Madeira is often
aged for many decades and is a
rare treat.

"Malmsey" is a British cor-
ruption of "Malvasia," and all
Madeira labeled "Malmsey" is, in
fact, made from Malvasia grapes.
Plan on spending around $15 for
your first Sercial Madeira.

Marsala

Named for the town on the western tip of
Sicily, Marsala is a brown-colored fortified
wine made from the green-skinned Catarralto
grape, a local variety. After harvesting, the

grapes are dried prior to fermentation, which raises the sugar level. After fortification, Marsala is often sweetened and darkened with grape juice syrup. Barrel-aging mellows its flavors.

Of all the fortified wines, Marsala is the least distinctive as a beverage and is best kept in the kitchen. Marsala comes in two styles, dry and sweet. Both are used for cooking.

Fortified Wines Worth Trying

1. *Very Dry Fino Sherry.* Recommended producer is Tio Pepé (Spain). Serve chilled, with appetizers.

2. *Amontillado Sherry.* Recommended producer is Savory & James (Spain). Drink it alone or with snacks. It tastes like